Ric Charlesworth coaches. Voted 'Co the last decade, hi Olympic Gold Me twice World Champions (1994, 1998) and eight times consecutively Number One in the world.

A four times Hockey Olympian, former first class cricketer, medical graduate and Federal Member of Parliament, Charlesworth has worked as a coaching consultant to sporting teams in Australian football, rugby and soccer as well as being employed as a mentor coach by the Australian Institute of Sport. He is a master coach appointed by the International Hockey Federation. He lives with his partner Carmen and their two children, Oscar and Hugo. He is also father to Kate, Libby and Jonathon. He is 52 years old.

This is Ric's third book. The best selling book *The Coach* was released in 2001 and *Staying at the Top* came out the following year. Ric's website is:

www.riccharlesworth.com.au

Also the author of:

The Coach: Managing for Success

Staying at the Top

Shakespeare
THE COACH

RIC CHARLESWORTH

Ric Charlesworth (signature)

PAN
Pan Macmillan Australia

First published 2004 in Pan by
Pan Macmillan Australia Pty Ltd
St Martins Tower, 31 Market Street, Sydney

Reprinted 2004

National Library of Australia cataloguing-in-publication data:

Charlesworth, Ric.
Shakespeare the coach.

ISBN 0 330 36478 2

1. Sports administration. 2. Sports sciences.
3. Sports – Psychological aspects.
4. Motivation (Psychology). 5. Leadership.
6. Management. I. Title.

796.077

Typeset in 11/15 pt Sabon by Post Pre-press Group
Printed in Australia by McPherson's Printing Group

I wrote this book while living in Cortona, a hilltop town in the South of Tuscany in late 2003 and early 2004. I should acknowledge the use of the Cortona Comune Library during that time.

Without the assistance of Carmen, my partner, the manuscript would never have been completed on time; and without the assistance of Oscar (3) and Hugo (1½) it would have been completed much, much earlier!

In 1623, when the First Folio of William Shakespeare's plays was published, Ben Jonson said this of his friend and fellow writer:

Thou art a Monument without a tomb
And art alive still, while thy booke doth live,
And we have wits to read, and praise to give

Contents

INTRODUCTION

In 2002, the French football team travelled to the Far East to defend their position as holders of the World Cup in football. They were also European Champions and within their ranks were the leading goal scorers in the English, Italian and French leagues – Thierry Henry, David Trezeguet and Djibril Cisse. The world's finest midfielder, Zinedine Zidane was also there, albeit not fully fit. As it turned out, despite this star-studded line-up, 'Les Bleus' did not win a single game or even score a goal, and were sent home after the first round.

The newspapers in France were scathing: 'a disastrously under-performing team'; 'Twisted and blinded by success and money, the players and those around them neglected the most important thing: the football field';

'They arrived in Asia, puffed up with pride and ambition and fell from a great height.' The French players were technically superior and tactically proven, but were they mentally ready, prepared and resilient? One can only presume that the answer to that question is no, for how else could they, given their pedigree, have mightily failed to progress to the next round?

As a coach taking a team into the Sydney Olympics in 2000, I too had endeavoured to ensure that a national team's earlier triumphs were repeated. As defending Olympic Champions and the World Cup holders, we had the pedigree, but the Olympic challenge was to get our heads 'right' for the task.

It's a general rule at any Olympic Games that the world champion or world record holder only wins one event in two or three. More than half the events produce upsets. Good past form does not ensure success, in other words, so players have to have their heads 'right'. I found many of the messages and the philosophy contained in the works of William Shakespeare were used to keep our team on track.

The chapters of this little book are full of the Bard's insights into the workings of our minds, and the relevance to coaching sporting teams or managing a business is clear. From leadership, strategy and teamwork to self-awareness, patience and resilience, there are invaluable guidelines that can assist you to get your team to perform at its best.

So what does Shakespeare have to offer the coach, manager, teacher or trainer?

. . . We are such stuff
As dreams are made on . . .

The Tempest, IV.i, lines 156–157

Prospero's reflective assertion to Ferdinand his prospective son-in-law is seen by many as Shakespeare's overt farewell to his art, in this *The Tempest*, one of his last plays. Those who lead, those who coach, direct and manage others do so best when they know where they are going. They have a purpose and a vision for their charges, team or organisation. Shakespeare knew as much and his body of work – massive, fluent, incisive and lasting – is testimony to that.

His works have been aptly described as 'the great book of life'. The themes are timeless revenge, love, corruption, ambition, success, failure, courage, compassion, war, suffering and mercy. And these are indeed the themes of life. Equally, many are the themes of sport, of competition, of challenge, and the search for success and achievement. Sport is great drama played on a stage where the athletes ad-lib and, if trained well, can work together to achieve their goals. The outcome is never known – except by some Indian and Pakistani bookmakers perhaps! It is played out before our eyes.

My aim is not to be a literary commentator, as there are so many better qualified than me to do so. What I hope to do in this book is to examine Shakespeare as a motivator, teacher, manager, observer, psychologist and student of human nature. To examine some of the things he wrote from the perspective of a coach, trainer or manager – one who takes the responsibility of getting his charges to realise their potential, to perform for their team or their company. Indeed, whatever the endeavour or wherever they ply their trade, these messages will apply.

It is the purpose that makes strong the vow

Troilus and Cressida, V.iii, line 23

Without a dream, a vision or purpose, most of us will drift along in the world. In a lifetime we meet some who inspire, provoke, catalyse or even direct and push us to focus our resources more effectively. Sometimes this person is a parent, family member, teacher, manager, coach, employer, friend, lover or partner. Their impact has the capacity to change our lives, our direction.

Some say we change, but this experience is often just a reorientation of priorities, resources, skills and abilities that we already possess. It is a reinvention of ourselves in which we recognise a grander or different purpose for ourselves, or we realise that we can perform at a much higher standard than at present. The experience can open up a pathway to achieve this new vision for ourselves or our group.

Harold Bloom is perhaps the world's most passionate and erudite lover of Shakespeare. In his wonderful book *Shakespeare: The Invention of the Human*, he proposes the idea that the Bard 'taught us to understand human nature'. He postulates further:

> Falstaff and Hamlet are the invention of the
> human, the inauguration of personality as we have

come to recognise it. The idea of Western character, of the self as a moral agent, has many sources: Homer and Plato, Aristotle and Sophocles, the Bible and St Augustine, Dante and Kant and all you might care to add. Personality, in our sense, is a Shakespearean invention, and is not only Shakespeare's greatest originality but also the authentic cause of his perpetual pervasiveness.

Bloom sees the influence of the Bard as the literary equivalent of the scriptures, and he argues that Shakespeare's influence on Western culture is, at least, as important as religion. 'He extensively informs the language we speak, his principal characters have become our mythology, and he, rather than his involuntary follower Freud, is our psychologist.' Bloom's enthusiasm at first overwhelmed me but as I have progressed with this project, I have become more and more convinced by his arguments.

I came to Shakespeare as a teenager studying Julius Caesar at school. Obligatory study and readings in the classroom were the catalyst for my attachment. Thirty-five years and numerous performances later, I found myself considering how I would share some snippets of Shakespeare's perspective with those who wish to teach, coach, manage and guide others.

When you coach a team you soon learn that each individual has different trigger points, is moved by different things, different stimuli, forces or motivations. The task of reaching everyone with the messages that you want to convey is indeed difficult. Much time is spent trying to find different ways to say something, different ways to convey the message so that it strikes a chord with the athletes.

The wisdom of the great philosophers, writers, poets and scholars, and of other coaches, as well as the experiences of athletes, past and present, are all part of the armoury of a coach. Over decades, I collected a vast array of such wisdom from a wide variety of sources wherever I could find them, and I use them to reinforce, repeat, inspire and vitalise those in the team.

What I found was that in most areas of human endeavour, Shakespeare had said something that was appropriate, touched a nerve and was relevant. In fact, he seemed to cover the spectrum better than anyone else.

While Shakespeare wasn't overly concerned with plots (indeed, most were stolen or quite facile), his great achievement is making his characters seem real. In describing indirectly their personalities and revealing their strengths and weaknesses, their follies, fantasies and foibles, he gave clues as to their motivations and laid down lessons, like epistles, on human folly and success.

Sports performance today covers a wide range of scientific, technical and tactical disciplines. Yet still the critical component in sport is the athlete and the area of greatest scope for improvement is in the mental approach – the mind.

For 'tis the mind that makes the body rich

The Taming of the Shrew, IV.iii, line 168

The beauty of Shakespeare's contributions was the timelessness, their authority, and the perceptiveness of such a large body of work. Shakespeare wasn't a sportsman – few were in his time. However, there are about 120 references to sport in his works. (Well, 'sport' referring mainly to hunting, gaming, joking and cavorting anyway!)

The idea of sport was one of distraction and diversion. Something light, relaxed and without the heavy burden of other matters, such as business or the law or war or the tedium of everyday life.

**What sport shall we devise here in this garden
To drive away the heavy thought of care?**

Richard II, III.iv, lines 1–2

Of course, to those participating or those close to it, modern sport is every bit as serious as business and the law – to some it is even as important as war. Whenever possible we have endeavoured to underline these parallels in this book.

Perhaps Shakespeare, always well ahead of his time, foresaw the demise of English cricket, on the back of the heavy schedule of professional county cricket . . .

**If all the year were playing holidays,
To sport would be as tedious as to work**

Henry IV, Part I, I.ii, lines 197–198

However, as a playwright and theatre company investor, he had a great involvement in the production of successful plays that were also enduringly popular. He worked hard to ensure quality and make the performance work. Shakespeare's theatre company had to function as a team competing with others to survive and prosper in Elizabethan London, so he understood very well the requirements of a competitive market and the necessity to operate effectively in such an environment.

Of course, Shakespeare has no comment on the physical preparation of athletes or the techniques of sport, but he has everything to say about the mind games of sport, and he touches on strategy and tactics in doing so.

He understands the need for people of action:

Talkers are no good doers . . .

Richard III, I.iii, line 351

He deals with team players and individuals, the effect of controlling your emotions, reliability, ambition, consistency, self-awareness, doubt and uncertainty, and resilience. All these attributes are part of the make-up of the best athletes and performers. Equally, his words talk to a coach, manager or leader about the exercise of his or her powers, persuasion, values, diligence, flexibility, strategy, purpose and direction.

I have endeavoured wherever appropriate to provide some indication or interpretation of Elizabethan language. In a similar way, many quotes have been cut down to underline the modern management context. Sometimes Shakespeare's context is completely different from that which I have tried to convey. In an exercise such as this, the difference is inevitable, yet it does not distract from the force of the message within the words.

Shakespeare was a great man of words but he was more a man of action, a practical theatre person more than an academic. His plays were written to be performed and were practical scripts open to interpretation. They proved robust enough to be commercially successful in their time and yet have also endured for centuries at the centre point of English literature.

The language perplexes; Elizabethan English and the inventiveness of the Bard can at times trouble our understanding, but when stripped down to the message then the meaning is clear. To coaches and managers, these timeless messages serve as reminders to their charges. They are often catalysts for action and progress – or, as Bloom put it, a 'system of Northern lights' that cannot be contained in playhouses and libraries, one with a pervasive presence and context.

In *Shakespeare the Coach*, we take Shakespeare to the locker-room or boardroom, and it is not out of place!

A Coach's Creed

They that have power to hurt and will do
   none,
That do not do the thing they most do
   show,
Who, moving others, are themselves as
   stone,
Unmoved, cold, and to temptation slow –
They rightly do inherit Heaven's graces,
And husband nature's riches from expense;
They are the lords and owners of their faces,
Others but stewards of their excellence

Sonnet 94, lines 1–8

Shakespeare wrote 154 sonnets that are effectively 'little songs', or lyrical poems of
fourteen lines. In the sixteenth century this
was a popular way to woo one's lover, and the
themes of his sonnets very much reflect love,

affection, rejection, sexual innuendo, and the emotions that accompany such concerns.

Perhaps the most enigmatic of all the sonnets is number 94, which seems to stand as a comment on the human condition of the archetypal 'leader'. The personality portrayed fits the outline of the leader or coach covered by much of the substance of this book. No reference is made in the sonnet to the speaker or the person addressed, as if the use of personal pronouns was being studiously avoided.

Some suggest, taken in the context of the more personal reflections in Sonnets 90 to 93, that it should sit in the context of a fickle youth capable of abandoning his pledges. But for me Sonnet 94 can stand alone. Certainly the first eight lines could serve well as what I call 'a coach's creed'.

The concepts dealt with here and resonating in the chapters of this book cover a range of coaching musts. Paraphrasing the above allows me to present one interpretation:

Use power wisely and do no harm.
Keep your strategy hidden and unpredictable.
Provide direction and persuade

While remaining objective and calm.
Do these things and rewards will come:
Your program will grow;
Your excellence will become the way
Of those under you.

The final six lines of the sonnet change the analogy to that of summer's flower, which is self-contained and in its time, sweet and beautiful. Given this vision of beauty and perfection, the worry is then expressed that if this thing becomes corrupted within, then even 'the basest weed' would not smell as bad. Sweet things if they turn sour, turn really sour – perhaps this is a dire warning for managers and coaches too!

The summer's flow'r is to the summer sweet
Though to itself it only live and die;
But if that flow'r with base infection meet,
The basest weed outbraves his dignity.
For sweetest things turn sourest by their
        deeds:
Lilies that fester, smell far worse than weeds

                    Sonnet 94, lines 9–16

Ten Favourite Quotes

1. He's truly valiant that can wisely suffer
   The worst that man can breathe,
   And make his wrongs his outsides

   Timon of Athens, III.v, lines 31–32

This quote reminds me of Kipling's 'If' in that it appeals to our ability to endure difficulties and keep our perspective and stay focussed. Coaching and managing at the highest level is not easy – it is demanding and stressful as good performances and results are expected. Even in those sports that don't have a lot of money tied up in the players and coaches, the desire to do well and achieve is still great.

Mostly the road to success is pitted with potholes and disappointments and there are inevitably times when all may seem lost or the program is off track. Equally, there will be criticism from those watching outside, and especially from those who are hoping you'll fail!

The ability to stay committed to the task and not become distracted or diverted is crucial if you are to ride out the storm. This is not to say that it may not be necessary to consider new options and look at alternatives; any manager worth his or her salary must be alive to change. The art is to balance flexibility, which should be ever present, with the patience and persistence of a religious zealot! That is not easy yet, as the Bard so eloquently put it, 'the slings and arrows of outrageous fortune' must be endured if you wish to be in the game.

2. Our praises are our wages; you may ride's
   With one soft kiss a thousand furlongs ere
   With spur we heat an acre . . .

   The Winter's Tale, I.ii, lines 94–96

My reputation was that of a hard task-master yet I was always aware of the need to reward the athletes as well as I could. Tangible rewards were resourced and provided from many sources. I believed assistance for the athletes was deserved and should be maximised. On the other hand, the excesses of professional soccer see players rewarded to an extent beyond what the game can afford. Hence in the UK about 90 per cent of professional clubs are insolvent, and eventually the soccer bubble must burst, with painful consequences for the majority of the players. Simply put, such practice is bad business.

Nothing can ever reward the athletes more than ultimate triumph as competitors in the major competitions, and becoming well-rounded individuals who realise their potential for their teams and themselves. These two goals are not mutually exclusive. Indeed by doing the latter you are well on the way to achieving the former.

Recently I was asked to speak on winning versus development as coaching priorities. My response was that in order to win you must develop, and in order to keep winning you must keep developing! They are concurrent aims.

By far the most important tool at the disposal of the coach or manager is to reward someone with approval and praise whenever it is earnt. Being 'present', interested, positive, sharply focussed and consistent is what this is about.

Many will say that handling highly paid, spoilt, petulant superstars is quite different but I do not accept this. A coach with faith in his or her judgement and consistent purpose and direction can build a program in which athletes, whatever their resources, understand the parameters and consequences of their actions. No athlete is beyond management and direction – even if the prescription may require moving them on!

National coaches, of course, have the option of appealing to such parameters as national pride in influencing their athletes. Those athletes for whom that does not work are probably better left out.

Shakespeare's advice is sound. Always praise good practices, habits, behaviours and approaches, and use the stick wisely . . . but know how and when to use it!

3. Thus did I keep my person fresh and new

Henry IV, Part I, III.ii, line 55

King Henry is describing how he managed the quest for power by keeping a low profile until he was ready to make his move. Coaches necessarily spend a lot of their time repeating and reinforcing their messages. Much of the stuff of teaching falls into this category and there is no way around it: only through a coach's constant insistence on excellent practices do the players develop the habits of quality and perfection that will serve them well over time and under pressure.

To continue to have an impact, those that manage are continually looking for new ways to present their ideas. New and exciting ideas come along yet the requirement to apply timeless principles remains. The best coaches are always looking for ways to reinvent and refresh themselves and better ways to communicate their ideas. If the athletes stop listening or aren't engaged, they will stop learning.

There are many ways to stay 'fresh and new' – you can use your assistants to share the load, engage ideas from other areas of life or sport, bring in new technologies or outside experts, etc. However, none of these things is a long-term solution. Rationing your efforts so as to maximise your impact, and keeping your 'powder dry' so that you time your interventions well, is part of the skill and art of coaching. Being rested and fresh is critical. It was thus in the time of Shakespeare just as it is today!

4. **Our doubts are traitors,**
   And makes us lose the good we oft might
      win
   By fearing to attempt . . .

   Measure for Measure, I.iv, lines 77–79

The message here is clear: you have to compete and overcome the burden of self-doubt if you are going to be successful. This quote is a favourite of mine because it is relevant to so many situations in everyday life. No coach ever knows the outcome of any match or contest in advance – the best teams and athletes can be beaten. For many it is their apprehensions that provide the fuel for their outstanding competitiveness.

The other side of this is the paralysing inertia of doubt that can make one risk-averse and indecisive. This great battle between belief and doubt is fought every time you compete against worthy opponents, and it is an ever-present obstacle to overcome.

The greatest win this battle most of the time but sometimes all of us fall short. When that occurs, the best competitors learn how to face the reality and continue on and upward.

Some, lamentably, are not able to do so, and therefore fail to realise their physical potential because they do not have the mental resources.

5. . . . the readiness is all . . .

Hamlet, V.ii, line 215

There are three things that are crucial to the success of your team or enterprise: preparation, preparation and preparation. In my view, Korea, Japan and the United States made the last eight in the 2002 World Cup because they prepared better than many of those with a much better pedigree. A number of those teams had a cursory preparation tucked onto the end of their heavy domestic seasons. In terms of building understanding, developing strategy and tactics, getting physically prepared and being a team, the preparation for the biggest event in their sport was perfunctory and inadequate.

My experience in Olympic preparation in

sports without such hype and profile was of far greater diligence, planning and attention to detail. Indeed, six to eight months (the sort of time Korea spent before the 2002 Finals) is required to be really ripe for such an event. Given that in club competitions the athletes often have many seasons developing their teamwork and methods, it is surprising that the international game doesn't recognise this need.

6. Men's faults do seldom to themselves appear

The Rape of Lucrece, 633

This is perhaps the raison d'etre of coaching. As analytical and self-aware as the best of us might be, there is always a place for an outside view or opinion on what we do. The coach can be a technical director and analyst, a strategist, a teacher and a motivator and adviser. The best are all of these things. The point made by the Bard is that all of us need to have someone holding the mirror up to our performances because we are not inclined to do it ourselves!

Like all of us, athletes avoid facing up to the truth about themselves where possible, and procrastinate and put off important business. The best coaches challenge such behaviour and do not allow their charges to fool themselves. Encouraging introspection in your athletes and assisting them to assess themselves in a mature way is a must.

We learn best from our mistakes, and those that manage and coach serve their charges best by being adept at delivering critical analysis. This is not the easy part of the job yet done well it plays a role in reinforcing learning and growth in individuals and the group.

7. . . . but 'tis a common proof
   That lowliness is young ambition's
      ladder,
   Where the climber-upward turns his
      face;
   But when he once attains the upmost
      round,
   He then unto the ladder turns his back,
   Looks in the clouds, scorning the base
      degrees
   By which he did ascend . . .

   Julius Caesar, II.i, lines 21–27

The story of the French soccer team in 2002 in the Introduction epitomises this message of complacency. Enduring champions are the really great performers, for they do not forget how they became great, and what they did to make it. There aren't that many of them, and we all know the contemporary ones: Gretsky in ice hockey; Armstrong in cycling; Sampras, Navratilova, Graf and Agassi in tennis; Tiger Woods in golf; Jordan in basketball; Lewis in athletics; Perkins and now Thorpe in swimming; Zidane, Ronaldo and maybe Hamm in soccer; and Wilkinson in Rugby Union.

This list is far from exhaustive but it tells a story of athletes who, once they achieved champion status, were able to sustain their performance. The key ingredients of such performers are great natural talent, a willingness to keep learning, an understanding of what was required to get there and a willingness to commit even more effort to maintain and improve performance.

To paraphrase the Bard, for every one of these champions there is a long list of those who 'once attaining the utmost round turned his back and looked into the clouds'. Too often we hear the tales of one-off champions whose careers were fleeting and whose fall from grace was rapid – as if they fell from Shakespeare's metaphorical ladder to the ground.

In team sport, as in many workplaces, with the requirement for complex integrated cooperation and coordination, the formula is even more difficult. Coaches wishing to succeed in building dynasties with their teams face the dilemma of our French football friends. Clive Woodward's outstanding two years will be a record-breaking run if he can extend it to retaining the next Rugby World Cup in 2007. In Australian football a fourth premiership for Brisbane in 2004 would rewrite the record book. Manchester United have built such a record recently in the English Premier League and Australia's cricketers are on the way to matching the dominance of the West Indies in the 1980s.

Success is seductive and for those that aspire to enduring greatness the seductress must be avoided. The focus should remain on the rungs of the ladder, not the clouds and the scenery. The consequence would likely be a fall, for 'Golden girls and lads all must, As chimney sweepers all come to dust.'

8. . . . in the very May-morn of his youth, Ripe for exploits and mighty enterprises

Henry V, I.ii, lines 120–121

The freshness, optimism, vitality and sheer ambition of young people are ingredients that every enterprise needs. That's not to say that this is the answer to all your problems. What is necessary is that you nurture young talent and develop a mix of youth and experience. Otherwise your team will be imbalanced.

James LeBron may only be the man-child fresh out of high school but he has been a great boost for the NBA's stock. Ian Thorpe no longer seems young given the emergence of Michael Phelps and his record-shattering year. Will Phelps attempt a Mark Spitz–like performance in Athens?

Every year we see emerging prodigies arrive to challenge the established order of things and every year young athletes, fresh and new are 'ripe for exploits and mighty enterprises'. The major league soccer season began in 2004 with a sellout crowd watching the debut of Freddy Adu. At 14 years old he is the youngest sporting pro in American history.

Recognising such talent and providing it

with opportunity when it is ready is the art of coaching and managing. Brash young tycoons often fail in business because of their youthful fervour as often as they succeed, and it is much the same in sport. One only needs to look at the tale of Anna Kournikova – promoted for the wrong reasons and without the requisite pedigree – to see how it can go wrong. While she may have been a marketing success she never really had it at tennis, I feel. The case of Serena Williams is in stark contrast to this: she had the athletic talent, and the marketing success followed as night follows day.

Teams are embellished by the injection of ambitious, talented youthful performers who set new goals. Indeed, these goals are often the records of the past and so new horizons come into focus. Accordingly the best teams can sustain their quality over time. Australia's all-conquering cricket team, now a very much ageing unit, will soon find themselves facing the challenge of renewal.

9. In them I trust, for they are soldiers
Henry VI, Part III, I.ii, line 42

Without trust, partnerships and teams fall apart – usually from within. This is not to say that management should not measure and challenge performance and practices, but an openness about direction, objectives and expectations is vital.

Equally, trust is a two-way street that requires management to genuinely engage contributions from your people and players.

As a coach your performance is reflected in the performance of your players, and their quality and commitment decides your fate, much like it does for a senior management executive in business. Of course the quality of your training, teaching, selection, tactics and motivation should impact on this! Then you have to trust that the players, or your employees will do justice to themselves and you.

In this quote, the Duke of York may be pretending to Henry's throne but he understands the trust factor. His men are trained soldiers ready for the task. He shows the same trust in them that present-day coaches show and feel every week when their teams go out to compete.

It is difficult to measure the worth of what

real teamwork can bring. The Korean team at the 2002 World Cup earnt altogether in a year about what David Beckham earns in a month, but that fact did not stop them progressing much further than more fancied rivals, including Beckham's team. I suspect that the six months they spent building their group in the lead-up to the Finals played an important part in that outcome. In the same way, in many businesses, the boss must trust his employees to be true to their training and provide the quality customer service that is crucial to a successful enterprise.

10. Plenty and peace breeds cowards; hardness ever
    Of hardiness is mother . . .

    Cymbeline, III.vi–(scene 6), lines 21–2

The best teams are full of 'fire fighters'; people who, faced with a problem, will find a way to solve it and actively get on with it. They know that the resources to solve their difficulties can be found within, and they have been trained to fix problems not flap about them!

Lance Armstrong is your classic 'fire

fighter', overcoming great obstacles to achieve success. Justine Henin-Hardenne's background was hardly idyllic yet she now stands at number one in women's tennis. And Hermann Maier resumed winning in 2003 after an accident that nearly cost him his leg and skiing career.

The resilient and resourceful turn 'diseases to commodity', as suggested by Falstaff in *Henry IV, Part II*, and overcome difficulties and obstacles. The experience makes them tougher and more resilient. Very often they eschew the smooth path for the rocky one and place themselves in situations where they are extended.

You can easily have a great win–loss record if you play easy opponents or fight below your weight. Truly competitive individuals challenge the best, sometimes being outclassed while they learn, but never run away from tough challenges.

CHAPTER 1

ACTION

Action is eloquence . . .

Coriolanus, III.ii, line 76

Volumnia is trying to persuade her son Coriolanus, a great warrior, to humble himself
before the people in the market place. She
suggests that going down on his knees will do
the trick.

Thy knee bussing the stones – for in such
    business   [bussing = kissing]
Action is eloquence, and the eyes of th'
    ignorant
More learned than the ears . . .

Coriolanus, III.ii, lines 75–77

Actions speak louder than words. She is sure that the sceptical crowd will be convinced by the kneeling gesture. The action will say it all.

In sport then, action is the name of the game. Coaches want people who, while cool, calculating and decisive, are capable of dynamic movement and actions – those who can put the theory into practice and achieve the outcomes required. The best strategy is pointless without the foot soldiers to do the deeds, win the ball, make the tackles and interceptions, defend, and score goals or points. Equally, your business requires people who solve problems, make decisions and act, and put good ideas into pragmatic working solutions.

The great challenge is to fulfil your promise in your chosen area. Whatever you may wish to do, and can conceive of doing, or plan, the task is to put it into practice. Philip, the illegitimate son of Richard the Lion Heart, is trying to strengthen John's resolve to stand and fight the French:

Be great in act, as you have been in thought

King John, V.i, line 45

King Harry (Henry IV) is anxious to get on with organising his forces on hearing that the rebels have met at Shrewsbury five days earlier. He realises that delay will whittle away his advantage and help his enemies.

Our hands are full of business. Let's away.
Advantage feeds him fat while men delay

Henry IV, Part I, III.ii, lines 180–181

Creative or instinctive

The time-honoured adage 'Don't think, act' has a place in sport. Very often the most brilliant technicians are those whose honed instincts and trained habits allow them to spontaneously perform. And very often there is little time for contemplation and consideration of the alternatives. What is needed is the immediate appropriate response to the stimuli presented.

Many people see the goal scorers in team ball sports as the 'creative people' but while this is a popular perception it is also a patently false one. Indeed, Ronaldo, van Nistelrooy, Henry and the like are actually instinctive operators whose speed, reflexes and instincts are their stock in trade; the creative 'decision makers' are further back, creating opportunity for these predators.

Even those who score through their 'spot kicking', such as a Lockett or Lloyd in Australian footy, Buchanan in gridiron, or even a Wilkinson in rugby, are people with automatic skills and routines. No decision making is entailed in their finishing – tunnel vision serves them best!

One of the most difficult issues in team ball sports is timing the stimuli that initiate the actions. The movement to receive the ball by the player without the ball is the thing that stimulates action and the delivery of the ball. Whether in basketball, football (soccer, rugby, Australian football or gridiron) or hockey, the timing is crucial. The player with the ball must see the movement, correctly select the option, and deliver the pass with perfect skill and execution.

Action distracted . . . inaction

Shakespeare was certainly not an aficionado of such games but he understood the concept.

Since things in motion sooner catch the eye Than what stirs not . . .

Troilus and Cressida, III.iii, lines 183–184

4

Here, Ulysses chides Achilles for his lethargy and indolence, for Achilles has been 'entombed' in his tent and not participating in the siege effort on Troy. Ulysses suggests that Achilles' great feats might be forgotten and his reputation lost if he does not come out and involve himself. So often in team sports an athlete can similarly be lost if he doesn't initiate and project himself into the game by his actions. How often have we heard it said that he or she 'just wasn't sighted out there today'?

The antithesis of action is a player or performer paralysed by fear or thinking too much. There is an optimal time for thinking but this has to be followed by action with purpose; action without purpose is just a waste of time. Inaction because of doubt or fear of consequences is fatal in sport and almost any other endeavour.

Shakespeare raises this many times (see Chapter 2, 'Doubts and Fears'). One example is in *The Winter's Tale* when Camillio is apologising to Leontes for his mistakes (although he's not sure yet what they are). Even the wisest, he says, sometimes are paralysed by fear into inaction:

... if ever fearful
To do a thing where I the issue doubted,
Whereof the execution did cry out,
Against the non-performance, 'twas a fear
Which oft infects the wisest ...

The Winter's Tale, I.ii, lines 258–263

While fear and doubt are one problem that can lead to delay and inaction, the other worry is thinking too much – being preoccupied with all the options and possibilities, or indeed pre-occupied with other matters. The outcome is similar: delayed action, or inaction.

Coaching lesson

Without decisive action and self-starting performers who take responsibility for what happens and for fixing problems, your organisation will be too slow-moving, rigid and non-responsive. Action is required at two levels:
1. automatic and instinctive; and
2. creative, decisive and flexible.

The greatest obstacle to such dynamic action is a mind burdened with irrelevant thoughts. The absence of irrelevant thoughts is what I call a state of optimal concentration.

CHAPTER 2

DOUBTS AND FEARS

Our doubts are traitors,
And makes us lose the good we oft might
 win
By fearing to attempt . . .

Measure for Measure, I.iv, lines 77–79

Measure for Measure deals with the moral issues of justice and mercy. Hypocrisy, civic corruption and infidelity are portrayed.

Isabella is talking with Lucio. Her brother Claudio has been sentenced to death in what appears to be a very harsh judgement. Isabella doubts she has the power to help but Lucio convinces Isabella not to be overcome by doubt, but to try to make a difference.

Shakespeare is raising a mirror to issues of

corruption and hypocrisy couched in a fanciful Viennese setting. (No doubt he had his eye on the good burgers of London at the time.) Again he broaches an issue that resonates through much of his work: that of the need to overcome our doubts and fears in order to achieve our aims, our purpose.

Similar wording appears in other plays. Perhaps given the superstitions of his time with the heavy hand of religious and metaphysical beliefs, it is not surprising. These concepts played an important part in the thinking of the populus, and Shakespeare, the contemporary playwright, was in touch with such sentiments.

In *Macbeth*, Lady Macduff expresses her concern as her husband has fled to England:

... **When our actions do not,**
Our fears do make us traitors

Macbeth, IV.ii, lines 3–4

Her cousin Ross, in reassuring her of her husband's nobility, reflects on the dangerous times:

But cruel are the times, when we are traitors
And do not know ourselves; when we hold
rumour

From what we fear, and yet know not what we fear

Macbeth, IV.ii, lines 18–20

These fears prove well founded, for Lady Macduff and her sons are murdered before the end of the scene.

Why do football teams so often play like lions at home and minnows away? What is the cause of such 'away from home' ineptitude? Clearly, it is a real phenomenon in most sports. Indeed, in soccer, goals scored away are actually valued more highly than home goals in the calculation of position in many competitions. In basketball, football and hockey throughout the United States, playing away hurts – statistics clearly identify this.

Principally, the cause is mental. While travel fatigue and environmental factors (like heat, altitude or ground conditions) can all play a part, it appears that what happens when playing away is that athletes and whole teams lose the struggle between doubt and belief. When things go wrong, as invariably occurs at some stage in any contest, the resilience and confidence of the individuals and/or group can become fragile. Belief loses out to doubts – doubts that are there in all of us.

Away from home, there is less external support in the form of the crowd. Indeed, they may be openly hostile. A parochial local crowd may sway umpiring decisions as well as making the task even more difficult, especially within the heads of the players. Athletes often try to deny and hide their doubts rather than facing them and seeing them for what they are – distractions that can cloud the mind, distort judgement and interfere with relaxed, free performance of skills. This is how our doubts can take over as 'traitors', making us indecisive, unsure and risk-averse.

Many of our doubts come from inside our heads. *Have we trained hard enough? Am I fit enough? Is the strategy correct? Can we come back from here? What if I miss this shot?* The best athletes learn to shelve such demons and focus on the task. This capacity is a skill, which is learnt at training and honed in competition. In the best competitors, it allows them to block out the outside world when under pressure.

It is no less so in business or life in general. Tough decisions are thus because the alternatives all have similar merit and whatever path is taken there will always be doubts as to the choice. Managing our doubts and accompanying fears, tests all of us every day.

Hamlet – probably Shakespeare's greatest character – was plagued by doubt and uncertainty. The mind games he suffers are instrumental in bringing him down. In the famous 'To be or not to be' soliloquy he gives expression to this question:

Thus conscience does make cowards of us all;
And thus the native hue of resolution
Is sicklied o'er with the pale cast of thought,
And enterprises of great pith and moment,
With this regard, their currents turn awry
And lose the name of action . . .

[Pith = importance]

Hamlet, III.i, lines 83–88

Hamlet was eventually inhibited by his negative thoughts and doubts, and unable to function usefully.

The Hamlet quote is close to one from gridiron coach Vince Lombardi, who said, 'Fatigue makes cowards of us all.' While Lombardi stressed that physical stress (tiredness) could induce corner-cutting, we can see the applicability of mental stresses also. Shakespeare clearly understood these things.

The best performers also allow fear of failure to work *for* them. The doubts outlined above can fuel our desire to train, prepare and compete. Respected opponents need not be feared. Indeed, they can be the catalyst for even better and more brilliant efforts.

Herb Elliot, Australia's greatest men's athlete of the twentieth century, was unbeaten in 44 races over 1500 metres and the mile. Elliot said he ran on his apprehensions – he trained hard to know he was prepared, and competed fiercely in order to assuage his doubts.

Coaching lesson

We all have doubts. We should acknowledge them and aim to overcome them in our training, preparation and competition. Let them work for you; know when to focus only on the task, and close down the mind to outside distractions, particularly our own thoughts. 'Don't think, act' is an old coaching adage that remains relevant today.

CHAPTER 3

EXCELLENCE

Things done well
And with a care exempt themselves from
    fear;
Things done without example, in their issue
Are to be fear'd . . .

Henry VIII, I.ii, lines 88–91

In the quote above, Henry is concerned that his taxation measures should not be the cause of civil unrest and so wishes to ensure that the measures will not be too punitive. (He even suggests pardons for those who cannot meet their payments!) The point is, he wants things done well.

Excellence is the commodity in which coaches like to deal. It is what underpins consistent performances. It's the habit created by training and honed by continual repetition that enables athletes to perform in pressure situations.

In my team I had only two rules that I insisted on at training: it had to be physically and mentally tougher, more complex and more demanding than the game. That way we were able to develop athletes who could deal with whatever came along. Their skills needed to be reproducible under pressure. That required really perfect technique and practice in conditions that exceeded those expected in the match.

The secret of consistent performance is developing excellent habits; and with care and attention to detail, such habits are created. But this does not come easily. It requires hard work, care and diligence to achieve greatness. Shakespeare makes this clear by suggesting that otherwise *everyone* would achieve or build greatness:

If to do were as easy to know what were good to do, chapels had been churches, and poor men's cottages princes' palaces . . .

Merchant of Venice, I.ii, lines 11–12

Portia makes the point here that it is much easier to tell or teach than to do. Indeed, actions speak much louder than words. Portia is frustrated by her father's deathbed decree that her husband would be chosen by lottery. It was easy for her father to decree it but she will have to live with the consequences!

Skills in sport appear effortless when performed well by champions; the champion seems to have time and always be ready for the next action or event. It's a great mistake to confuse this quality we see in champions with the idea that the skill is easy. While the actual stroke or action may be simple in conception, the great difficulty is being able to reproduce it, repeatedly, in the right place at the right time for the right purpose. Such timing and achievement is never easy.

While we see the excellence of performance that results from training our bodies, our technique and our skills, it is worth remembering that it is the power of the mind that wills us to such levels of perfection.

> . . . Our bodies are our gardens to the which
> our wills are gardeners . . .
>
> *Othello*, I.iii, lines 320–321

In this speech, Iago is advising Roderigo about his passion for Desdemona and the need to control his passion with his mind. We are able to nurture our will to work hard. 'Idleness' will render the garden sterile, yet 'industry' can manure the crop. In the same way, we will ourselves to excellence through our industriousness and diligence.

Excellence through essence

Perhaps the most important discovery that we can make in life is to discover our essence, to discover the thing that brings us alive and that most defines our being. Each of us has the capacity to excel at something yet may pass through life without ever discovering – or even worse, without pursuing – their talents. Few achieve excellence in things that they aren't truly attached to, engrossed in and in love with.

Shakespeare understood the essence of things, so much so that he travelled to London, where he immersed himself in the theatre and left for us the marvellous legacy of his work.

What's in a name? That which we call a rose By any other word would smell as sweet

Romeo and Juliet, II.i, lines 43–44

To Juliet, it matters not that Romeo is a Montague, and therefore the sworn enemy of her family, the Capulets. She loves him because of what he is – his *essence* – just as we can love art, music, sport or even mathematics. The real secret of succeeding in life is being able to discover and pursue these things. Then the travail is not drudgery but joy.

Similarly, Mark Antony is a great warrior – it is his raison d'etre (besides Cleopatra), and he rises early and enthusiastic for the fight with Caesar. The contest offers him the chance to pry his talent and test his skills as a commander and warrior. Again, essence is the key:

To business that we love we rise betime, and go to't with delight   [betime = early]
Antony and Cleopatra, IV.iv, lines 20–21

The really great athletes are great trainers. They work hard at perfecting their skills and you don't hear them complaining about the time spent doing so. My experience was that I could lose myself in the game or practice to the extent that outside worries and troubles were distant, forgotten and unimportant.

Excellence brought absorption, release and freedom not found anywhere else.

In *Othello*, Iago is forever advising and directing Roderigo while scheming to bring down Othello. He suggests to Roderigo that he allow some time to pass while waiting for his chance. While the context might not fit exactly, the sentiment is valid, as time always seems to pass swiftly when we are engrossed in our favourite activities.

Pleasure and action make the hours seem short

Othello, II.iii, line 367

Coaching lesson

The best coaches and managers know what excellence is, and insist on it unconditionally and continuously. This is sometimes a hard deal to sell as it entails hard work and real commitment. However, once the ethos is established and the mindset of quality becomes the essence of the organisation, then there is a certain self-fulfilling inevitability about it: anyone absorbed in fulfilling their potential can lose themselves in the task.

CHAPTER 4

HUMILITY

It is the witness still of excellency
To put a strange face on his own perfection
Much Ado About Nothing, II.iii, lines 43–44

Much Ado About Nothing is a play best known for the love–hate relationship of Beatrice and Benedick, which runs parallel to the traditional story of love between Hero and Claudio, and its machinations. Beatrice and Benedick display coolness and witty detachment as their defence against their innermost feelings. In the end this zany comedy all works out.

This little pearl on humility comes as Don Pedro, the Prince of Aragon, entreats his attendant Balthasar to sing some more. Balthasar protests that his voice is not good enough to 'slander music any more than once', to which Don Pedro replies:

It is the witness still of excellency
To put a strange face on his own perfection.
I prey thee sing, and let me woo no more

Much Ado About Nothing, II.iii, lines 43–45

Like a number of the quotes used in this book, the philosophical message here may not be seminal to the play, but its truth and applicability to human endeavour and its reflection on human nature are clear. In his insightful book *Good to Great*, Jim Collins examines what makes companies great. Collins' analysis shows empirically that the companies that do best are led by humble and determined CEOs. The highly paid, high profile, noisy bosses are not the ones who take good businesses to great performances.

There is a common misconception that brash, confident, even arrogant demeanour is the stuff of champion sporting performers. In my view, nothing could be further from the truth. The best performers and performances are born in an environment of genuine humility, and that accompanies a desire to continually improve and add to what you already have achieved. Champions are seldom satisfied with one triumph or victory; they are in search of perfection and longevity in the activity closest to their hearts. To wit: Lance Armstrong seeks a sixth Tour de France victory; Schumacher chases a sixth driver's championship; Tiger Woods would surpass Nicklaus; the Australian cricket team wants to dominate everyone; the Brisbane Lions seek a fourth consecutive premiership that would rewrite record books; and Manchester United and Real Madrid strive for continual dominance in their respective leagues and in Europe.

There are many characteristics that define champion teams and performers, but one of the most indispensable is a humility underpinning an approach that says, 'I can do better . . . there is more to do . . . we can improve.' This willingness to learn and desire to further improve, and the drive to do so, underpins a diligent approach to training, preparing and adding to your repertoire. It also speaks of a disciplined lifestyle and a mentality that never cuts corners and always ensures quality performances.

Champions allow their deeds to speak for them and concentrate their energies on improving rather than publicising their excellence or achievements. Indeed, such humility and lack of bravado is an essential element, I believe, in being ready to learn and receive new information and ideas.

There is, of course, another utility in such humility. One is able to avoid, as much as possible, the attention of others, and often enjoys the advantage of being underestimated. The 'dark horse' element is not available to the famous and vocal performer who draws attention to themselves.

What great ones do the less will prattle of

Twelfth Night, I.ii, line 33

Shakespeare, the observer of human nature, touched on these ideas in many of his works. He warned about those who are puffed up with pride and enjoy the flattery of others:

He that loves to be flattered is worthy o' th' flatterer

Timon of Athens, I.i, lines 229–230

Humility is the starting point of this improvement. Quiet, workmanlike, well-prepared performers are those capable of great performances, and are more likely to produce them. Of course, the natural gifts that are crucial to sporting prowess (speed, strength, coordination) are seldom enough to secure success; it is the *embellishment* of these gifts that makes the great champion. It is unusual to see this occurring unless the athlete or performer is willing to acknowledge and embrace the need to keep improving (and adds further layers of excellence).

Shakespeare repudiates the vice of pride that is often raised in his characters. Too often, successes breed a complacency and a lack of acknowledgement of the sources and methods of such achievement. Coaches must be forever vigilant to the excess of self-delusion that come with goals achieved and contests won.

The downfall of many a team and athlete, and of many a business, has followed a particular success, or an outstanding performance, which when achieved is seen as an end in itself. Often the easiest part of performance is the initial quest for excellence, fuelled by great ambition and purpose. Just as Caesar was told to beware the Ides of March, coaches and managers ought to be wary when ambitions are fulfilled. This is where those too easily satisfied and lacking humility forget how they became good in the first place!

In *Julius Caesar*, Brutus is unable to sleep and so muses in his orchard, pondering the possibility of Caesar becoming larger than life, a virtual living god in Rome, and the prospects that this might bring to his beloved Rome. Brutus is making a case in his own mind for the violent actions that will bring the Emperor down. He considers that ambition once fulfilled replaced by pride and self-love are very dangerous. He is convincing himself that this is Caesar's folly:

. . . But 'tis a common proof
That lowliness is young ambition's ladder,
Where the climber-upward turns his face;
But when he once attains the upmost
   round,
He then unto the ladder turns his back,
Looks in the clouds, scorning the base
   degrees
By which he did ascend . . .

Julius Caesar, II.i, lines 21–27

24

The message is clear to all who wish to achieve excellence in what they do, whether in sport or work or relationships. Always remember what made you succeed in the first place, practise it, improve it and keep it clear as a pathway to continued development. If you lose sight of that, you can be assured your fall from grace will be ahead of you.

The final word on humility comes from King Henry IV while still concerned at his son Prince Hal's development and readiness to assume the throne. He offers advice about leadership that is as true today as then:

And then I stole all courtesy from heaven,
And dress'd myself in such humility
That I did pluck allegiance from men's
    hearts,
Loud shouts and salutations from their
    mouths

Henry IV, Part I, III.ii, lines 50–53

Coaching lesson

Humility is the seed of continued excellence. Beware of vanity and overconfidence, for humility is also the seed of continued improvement. Ambition achieved ought never signal a loss of appreciation of how it was achieved. If you lose sight of that, your fall can be quick as Caesar's!

There is a pragmatic benefit in humility that bears consideration. Coaches and managers need the emotional maturity and skill to nurture cooperation and unity, and the example they set in this area can usefully infect the attitudes and behaviours of the whole group. As a leadership style, there is much to recommend understated, yet firm, belief and confidence.

CHAPTER 5

LEADERSHIP – PURPOSE AND PERSUASION

The speciality of rule hath been neglected

Troilus and Cressida, I.iii, line 78

Ulysses laments the fragmentation that has occurred in the Greek camp during the seven-year siege of Troy. Where leadership falters, discipline, order and harmony have been eroded and morale is low. Even the great Achilles idles away his time without direction or purpose.

Shakespeare knew leadership was as difficult as it was crucial to success in an endeavour. Good leadership sets the foundation for any effort as it fuels endeavour and motivates. It is the stuff that gives direction, vision, purpose and meaning. The best leaders not only know where they are going they are able to *persuade* others to follow. It truly is as Shakespeare says, a 'speciality'.

So what does Shakespeare have to say about giving purpose and direction? What does he have to offer about a leader's ability to persuade?

In *King Henry IV, Part II*, Lord Hastings, one of the rebels opposing Henry, makes his point to Lord Bardolph while planning action against Henry with the Archbishop of York and Lord Mowbray. He wants the men to have direction and hope:

. . . it never yet did hurt
To lay down likelihoods and forms of hope

Henry IV, Part II, I.iii, lines 33–34

The flip side of honest planning and laying out of your purpose is put very clearly by Lear's loving daughter Cordelia. She suggests some are not to be trusted:

. . . that glib and oily art
To speak and purpose not . . .

King Lear, I.i, lines 224–225

Cordelia refuses to say other than what she means despite the consequences!

The best teams and companies have mission statements and sets of values that underpin their direction and their way of doing things. The reinforcement and encouragement of such values in setting goals and direction for the organisation gives *purpose* to the group and individuals. It is a powerful motivating force.

You need not have the most concrete of goals. The great leaders set goals never before achieved and then set out to do what others deem impossible. So it is that:

. . . **We are such stuff as dreams are made on** . . .

The Tempest, IV.i, lines 156–157

The more difficult the goal, the greater the quest, and the more problematic the outcome will be. However, without such purpose seldom are great advances made or is new territory explored for better ways to do things.

Purpose
Sometimes, of course, the purpose might be a false one. Then, real flexibility might be

required to readjust one's vision. When the reason for action is not convincing, change your mind and pull out!

It is the purpose that makes strong the vow;
But vows to every purpose must not hold

Troilus and Cressida, V.iii, lines 23–24

Here, Cassandra is trying to persuade her brother Hector not to go to battle, but the tragic hero believes he will be fighting for his honour, which is more dear to him than anything else:

Life every man holds dear, but the dear man
Holds honour far more precious dear than
    life

Troilus and Cressida, V.iii, lines 27–28

For Hector, to not turn up would be a great dishonour. Cassandra, his wife Andromache, and his father are unable to convince him not to go. They are unable to convince him that his honour is a hollow purpose in this case – it will serve no good. Tragically, Hector is slain by a group of Achilles' thugs in an unfair and dishonourable contest.

The best coaches and managers have the capacity to convince their charges of the worth of their task, mission or goal. Athletes without a sense of purpose or belief are erratic, directionless and often lack the drive to work, prepare, compete and rebound from disappointments. Convincing others of the vision and direction to be taken is a crucial part of the task, and it is only by giving meaning and direction that the best results can be achieved.

Shakespeare understood that the cause of 'honour' was often more about pumped-up pride than about utility. The emptiness of Hector's quest for honour is clear to Cassandra and others, but in his stubbornness Hector cannot be changed.

Elsewhere, Shakespeare uses Falstaff, one of his greatest characters, to again illustrate the point that honour is never a good enough reason to lose one's life. Sir John Oldcastle (Falstaff) is not below pretending to be killed in battle in order to survive the fray. He rises from 'being dead' to announce:

. . . The better part of valour is discretion; in the which better part I have saved my life

Henry IV, Part I, V.iv, lines 118–120

Shakespeare would argue for strong, rational reasons for actions. Such purpose supports our best endeavours and helps to ensure that our resources are optimally utilised.

Persuasion

This task of convincing, directing and persuading requires vision and the capacity to lay down a pathway or roadmap underpinned by a believable vision and modus operandi. The capacities of Shakespeare's characters to persuade with reason, rhetoric and hope are legendary, and Mark Antony's speech over the body of Caesar is a landmark example of such skills:

Friends, Romans, countrymen, lend me your
   ears;
I come to bury Caesar, not to praise him.
The evil that men do lives after them;
The good is oft interred with their bones;
So let it be with Caesar. The noble Brutus
Hath told you Caesar was ambitious.
If it were so, it was a grievous fault;
And grievously hath Caesar answer'd it.
Here, under leave of Brutus and the rest –
For Brutus is an honourable man;

So are they all, all honourable men -
Come I to speak in Caesar's funeral.
He was my friend, faithful and just to me;
But Brutus says he was ambitious,
And Brutus is an honourable man.
He hath brought many captives home to Rome,
Whose ransoms did the general coffers fill;
Did this in Caesar seem ambitious?
When that the poor have cried, Caesar hath
    wept;
Ambition should be made of sterner stuff.
Yet Brutus says he was ambitious,
And Brutus is an honourable man

Julius Caesar, III.ii, lines 73–94

Antony sets out to turn the people against Brutus and the other assassins but must use subtlety to win over the audience, as Brutus has status and is respected in Rome. Using repetition and by cynically describing 'the honourable men' in juxtaposition with Caesar's good deeds, he gradually wins over the crowd. He is self-deprecating; he paints an image of Caesar's decency; he reads Caesar's will (favourable to the people) to persuade the crowd of the folly of the Emperor's death . . . all the while describing Brutus and Cassius as 'honourable men'. It is a brilliant piece of persuasion.

Of course, rhetoric is not the only route to persuasion. Nothing is more effective than truth and honesty. As Queen Elizabeth I says to rebuke a fawning Richard!

An honest tale speeds best being plainly told

Richard III, IV.iv, line 358

So tell it plainly and keep it simple. In *Hamlet*, Polonius had plenty of advice for those around him. Perhaps this was his best piece of advice:

. . . brevity is the soul of wit

Hamlet, II.ii, line 90

Often the coach must appeal to the better nature of his or her charges, or indeed lead the group in gaining the self-awareness and self-insight that are so crucial to define our raison d'etre (our purpose).

The silence often of pure innocence
Persuades when speaking fails

The Winter's Tale, II.ii, lines 41–42

Here, Paulina is hopeful that the sight of the King's newborn daughter might soften his jealous and misplaced anger against Hermione, his wife, whom he has wrongfully jailed for adultery. The message holds true that often the best course of action is to allow contemplation to work through the issue.

As a leader you are often keen to tell people what to do, to point out faults or persuade through your reasoned arguments. Sometimes the best course of action is to raise the issue and then let it dwell in silence while the group or individual considers the detail. Never be too quick to give the answer or your account. Allow others to participate and draw conclusions. Silence is a powerful tool that many are uncomfortable with, yet solutions and truths that emerge through reflection and contemplation carry much more weight than answers or solutions given by the boss!

Use power wisely

What else can Shakespeare offer on leadership? Many of his powerful leaders are flawed. Antony likes the good life too much, Othello suffers proud jealously, Lear cannot interpret the truth around him, and Richard II is vain and capricious in mixing with fools.

> **The skipping King, he ambled up and down**
> **With shallow jesters and rash bavin**
> **   wits,**   [bavin = brushwood]
> **Soon kindled and soon burnt; carded his**
> **   state,**   [carded = debased]
> **Mingled his royalty with cap'ring fools**
>> *Henry IV, Part I*, III.ii, lines 60–63

Henry IV who wins Richard's throne is contrasted for his sober and balanced humble approach

> **Thus did I keep my person fresh and new**
>> *Henry IV, Part I*, III.ii, line 55

Indeed, any leader needs to know when to use his position and power, and how to use it without overdoing it or abusing it. As leaders, coaches are required to give the same message over a period of time, and keeping yourself 'fresh and new' is part of the craft and art of persuasion. Clearly, Shakespeare understood this well.

Coaching lesson

One of the purposes of this book is to provide resources from another time and place to reinforce many of the messages of performance and the modern psychology of sport. Four centuries ago, Shakespeare interpreted and described the motivations and methods of human interactions in a way that should awaken our awareness of these influences today. He understood the role of leaders in giving purpose and direction, both moral and obligatory. He describes how failed leadership could lead to disharmony and calamity. He understood the art of persuasion through example, rhetoric, directness and at times by awakening self-awareness.

Chapter 6

LEARNING, CHANGE

O this learning, what a thing it is!

The Taming of the Shrew, I.ii, line 156

Gremio, the rich yet ageing suitor of Bianca, bemoans light-heartedly that he might not be able to woo her as cleverly as a better educated person. He employs Lucentio to tutor Bianca, not knowing that Lucentio also has designs on her. The point of this quote is to value learning, growth and betterment – it can make a difference to your chances!

The best workplaces are also learning places and training centres, just as the best teams in sport dwell in a place where learning, growth and training are central to the ethos and structure. This does not occur automatically, it requires a deliberate, conscious approach by the coach.

Many, in modern sport look to 'buy the best' in order to succeed (viz Manchester United, Real Madrid and Chelsea). Yet for many others, such an approach is not possible, nor advisable. That may be because of budgetary constraints within the organisation, or it may not be possible because of the parameters of the competition (salary caps, draft rules) or for international teams' citizenship requirements.

However, more important than any of the above is that to differentiate yourself from others, you should aim to add value to your people and stamp your principles, values, ideas and habits on them. This task is the most difficult in many ways, yet it can be the most effective, satisfying and enduring route to building a great team.

Those that come to your team or organisation come with a huge variety of skills, abilities, attitudes and attributes. Many are very confident in their capabilities yet many will have poor habits and work practices, and little insight into their real capacities. Shakespeare knew this very well!

The Rape of Lecrece was the Bard's second poem, published little more than a year after the runaway hit *Venus and Adonis*. These poems first showed his skill as a dramatist and both were reprinted several times in Shakespeare's lifetime. Tarquin, the son of the King, rapes the chaste and defenceless Lucrece and brings shame on his family, who are driven out of Rome.

While struggling with the Prince, Lucrece tries to persuade him of his folly but Tarquin is overcome by lust. He knows where his act will lead but cannot help himself. Lucrece entreats:

**Men's faults do seldom to themselves
    appear;
Their own transgressions partially they
    smother:
This guilt would seem death-worthy in thy
    brother**

The Rape of Lucrece, lines 633–635

The best programs must set about utilising and embellishing talents to the benefit of the team or organisation. This entails correcting faults eradicating sloppy habits and ensuring quality and excellence. It requires new skills to be taught and certainly means that the values of your organisation will become those of the new employee, or team member.

In sport this process may take many years, and in the end it often isn't possible and so a player may move on elsewhere. I suspect that in most businesses, less attention is paid to this learning development process, but it is no less critical to maximising the potential of your organisation.

This process is not easy, as it requires *change* and often *criticism* of former ways and methods. Done well, it requires a broadening of horizons yet at the same time a certain introspection is necessary to truly see oneself and to recognise faults and acknowledge past mistakes. In highly paid, pampered athletes and executives, the task can be Herculean! Sometimes their resistance is borne of insecurity, and they are extremely sensitive to criticism or analysis of their performance. Others are superficial believers of their minders and protectors, and have succeeded because of physical and technical skills that are largely unthinking and beyond analysis. The best humbly seek further improvement, and desire to learn and grow to realise the limit of their potential.

Changing our preconceptions, being more flexible is the stuff of real emotional maturity.

Here Benedick is changing his earlier views on marriage!

> . . . I did never think to marry. I must not seem proud; happy are they that hear their detractions and can put them to mending

Much Ado About Nothing, II.iii, lines 216–218

Good businesses and successful teams work aggressively to change for the better the practices, demeanour and the ways of their people. They find methods to approach those who procrastinate and avoid, those who hide. The coach or manager must endeavour to be seen as an objective expert who can play a part in the performer's development. This is seldom easy.

Employees who have been a long time ensconced and already have status, or are reluctant to change, can be hard to shift. Many professional athletes are used to being told how great they are by the cheering herd, many are obscenely remunerated, and don't like criticism. Even the semi-professional will have the experience of adulation, and many have developed a robust defence against criticism of their ways and performance.

Shakespeare, of course, had much to say on these matters, which are central to how a society and individuals learn and develop. They are central to the personality and performance of us all. So, what are the lessons?

Take responsibility

Our remedies oft in ourselves do lie,
Which we ascribe to heaven . . .

All's Well That Ends Well, I.i, lines 202–203

Here, a lowborn orphan, Helena, decides to pursue the reluctant and out-of-reach Bertram. (Eventually her persistence pays off after a multitude of machinations!) The point made is that only by taking action ourselves, rather than trusting fate, can we achieve our aims. Light-hearted though the action may be, Shakespeare underlines the need for us to take responsibility for our lives.

Learn from your mistakes:

There is a whole raft of quotes from the Bard that encourages introspection about performance and reinforce the need for us to learn from our mistakes. It is a timeless message, one that is heavily resisted, for the first requirement is for us to admit to errors or faults. This can be very difficult!

The best way to effect change in any environment is to get those involved working on it: to get them working on themselves. It's an inside job, and Shakespeare knew it! Once you start to make progress, you find a group who embrace learning and change, and acknowledge their errors.

In *Measure for Measure*, Mariana is in love with the flawed Angelo and is willing to forgive him his trespasses. Angelo has behaved heinously but is repentant; luckily he is saved and ends up with the forgiving Mariana. While Angelo is far from the best of men in Mariana's eyes, she thinks he can be resurrected!

They say best men are moulded out of faults;
And, for the most, become much more the
better

Measure for Measure, V.i, lines 437–438

The first step to improvement is to acknowledge errors and make a commitment from inside to change. The process of learning and changing receives much attention from Shakespeare. His characters were mostly flawed in some way, and much work was required to redeem them!

Coaching lesson

The process of change is difficult. It is best effected by those who are honestly self-aware, humble enough to want to keep improving, and willing to take responsibility for their actions and learn from their errors.

CHAPTER 7

MIND OVER MATTER

. . . Present fears
Are less than horrible imaginings

Macbeth, I.iii, lines 136–137

For 'tis the mind that makes the body rich

The Taming of the Shrew, IV.iii, line 168

In the first of the quotes above, a troubled Macbeth has just heard from the witches of his future prospects, and one of their prophecies is quickly realised. Macbeth is a little spooked by the 'supernatural soliciting'. The second quote sees Petruchio insisting to Kate that fine clothes don't make one rich, that the quality of one's thoughts are more important. Many of Shakespeare's characters are troubled by thoughts and worries to the point that they are unable to function properly. The power of the mind in determining our fates and actions is a constant theme.

We have investigated the part of doubts and fears as an area for coaching and management; objectivity, patience, resilience and self-awareness are also themes where thoughts and passions can interfere with performance, and each is covered in later chapters. In this chapter we look at a collection of reflections, by Shakespeare's characters, on the question of the mind's role in determining our effectiveness in functioning.

The age-old bug bear of performing under pressure is anxiety. In wanting to do well, we often try too hard and lose our composure and fluency. Muscles tighten up and thoughts of consequences and outcomes take over from task orientation that serves us best.

Striving to better, oft we mar what's well

King Lear, I.iv, line 347

In this context, Albany is advising Goneril against greed, but the sentiment holds: trying too hard can bring you down. Our inability, when distracted, to see things as they are is one of the great problems that coaches face. How do you get your athletes to focus without being influenced by the outside issues? Our mind can play tricks on us, as Troilus observes:

Fears make devils of cherabuns; they never see truly [cherabuns = angels]

Troilus and Cressida III.ii, lines 66–67

Of course, when it comes to performing up to standard or meeting expectations the same problems arise. Things are seldom as easy to perform as they appear to be or as we imagine them to be in our minds. It is easier to propose or consider courses of action than it is to actually get on with them: 'Be great in act, as you have been in thought.'

A similar sentiment is expressed by Poins in *Henry IV, Part II*:

Is it not strange that desire should so many years outlive performance?

Henry IV, Part II, II.iv, lines 250–251

Okay, so the speaker here is commenting on the elderly Falstaff in action with his whore, but still, this is also the timeless issue that the ageing champion must face in sport. There is no symmetry in the decline of the physical and mental faculties. The ageing champion knows what to do, where to go, but can no longer conjure up the physical resources to get there and do as he desires. This disconnection between the mind and body is often resisted and denied. Astute coaches and managers should be ever vigilant about recognising such developments in their people.

As usual, it remains for *Hamlet*, Shakespeare's greatest play, to provide the best-remembered quotes on the issue of mind and matter. Hamlet, the relativist, showing signs of his state of mind, jousts with Rosencrantz and Guildenstern about whether being in Denmark is like being imprisoned:

. . . for there is nothing either good or bad,
but thinking makes it so.
To me it is a prison

Hamlet, II.ii, lines 248–250

'Life is how you take it' could be one reading of this but the flakiness of Hamlet's moral values is outlined in this comment. (It is the sort of thinking that might justify murder!) Cultural relativism can lead to a slippery slope of amoral behaviour, but it does say something about the power of the mind to control actions and justify almost anything.

Finally, Ophelia, her father killed by Hamlet (her lover), rants in madness:

> . . . They say the owl was a baker's daughter.
> Lord, we know what we are, but know
> not what we may be . . .
>
> *Hamlet*, IV.v, lines 40–42

The first phrase here is difficult to understand but it does give an indication of her state of mind. It probably refers to an old legend of the daughter who offered a miserably small piece of bread to Christ and was turned into an owl for her meanness. In Elizabethan times 'the baker's daughter' also alluded to harlotry and loose behaviour.

However, there is real meaning to the second half of the quote. Knowing 'what we may be' is at the heart of coaching and management. Coaches help to set out a vision and goals, which though difficult, may be achievable; and for everyone in the team, the coach spends energy endeavouring to get them there. Knowing what you can become and what you are capable of achieving is essential to success in sport, as it is in any enterprise. On the other hand, Ophelia, snug in the privileged yet ruthless environment of the Danish court, has seen her safe world collapse around her and her final resort is to commit suicide. She is lost, frightened and alone, and very uncertain about what will become of her.

While this outcome appears very melodramatic, even outside the world of fiction the reality for those without purpose and direction can be very confusing and difficult. Quality leadership and coaching can help avoid this. Having a 'mind's eye view' of where you are going and what will be achieved is essential, and the mind's connection with the goal is essential. So much so that the mind can help make the 'matter' come true.

Coaching lesson

The mind is the driver of performance much more so than any other factor: it is our internal drive and the volition that determines our progress. Whether your self-talk is positive or negative can influence your belief and purpose. Similarly, too much thinking and worrying and anxiety can debilitate, whereas controlled and directed thoughts underpin a career that realises its potential.

CHAPTER 8

OBJECTIVITY

Make boot of his distraction, never
  anger   [boot = bounty, advantage]
Made good guard of itself

Antony and Cleopatra, IV.i, lines 8–9

Caesar laughs at Antony's challenge to personal combat. Maecenas, one of Caesar's followers, suggests here that Antony, distracted by anger at Caesar's refusal, is likely to be careless and make mistakes of which Caesar's men can take advantage.

Aristotle said it is okay to get angry about events so long as it is with the right person or thing, at the right time, for the right reason, to the right degree, for the right purpose. He was arguing that there is a place for emotion –

even anger – but it ought to have utility, purpose or meaning. The great danger in strong emotions like love, anger, hatred, and so on, is that they have the capacity to derail reason.

Sporting contests are exciting and emotional because of their unpredictability. However well-prepared and skilled your team may be, there is no way of predicting the outcome when the opponents are closely matched. There are no certainties when the competition is fierce and determined.

At the Olympic Games, as stated earlier, fifty to sixty percent of events see World Champions or world record holders defeated. The uncertainty that goes along with such competition breeds tension, stress, adrenalin and emotional involvement. Managing that emotion is a crucial part of optimising performance.

Coaches and managers, like athletes and employees, need the capacity to be analytical, cool and dispassionate in the heat of battle when things can be chaotic, confusing and difficult. The old saying is: 'Anger makes you stupid.' We aren't at our rational best when high emotions are playing on our thoughts and distracting us. Along with anger, anxiety, tension, joy, fear and frustration are all things that can operate to distract us from our tasks.

We have already looked at the distraction caused by fear and doubt but that really is just a subset of the greater issue that affects us performing our duties. Managing our overall emotional state is central to our being able to function optimally when it counts.

Hamlet recognises the quality of objectivity that he would like in his associates:

... Give me that man
That is not passion's slave, and I will wear him
In my heart's core, ay, in my heart of heart

Hamlet, III.ii, lines 69–71

The Prince of Denmark is looking for those who can best judge the guilt or innocence of his Uncle Claudius, whom Hamlet suspects has killed his father to usurp the throne. Later in the same scene, *Hamlet*'s players are performing a parody of his predicament entitled 'The Mousetrap'. Similar sentiments are spoken, this time by the player king:

What to ourselves in passion we propose,
The passion ending, doth the purpose lose

Hamlet, III.ii, lines 189–190

While *Hamlet*'s context might be different, this sentiment is timeless and holds as a principle to guide us through life. Too often, hasty decisions made when flooded by emotion are not wise. Coaches and managers (indeed, all of us in everyday life), need to balance reason and emotion so we don't fall into this trap.

Selective abstraction

Selective abstraction is the fault of seeing what we want to see – that which fits our preconceptions or appetite rather than being an accurate or true reflection of what is going on. Seeing what *is*, not just what we want to see, is crucial if we are going to make good judgements.

Indeed, this is one of the most common mistakes that coaches and managers make. It is something that I try very hard to avoid, although it's easy to see how it occurs.

A player that the coach insisted on having, but who now may not be performing well, is sometimes viewed more favourably by the coach (wanting to be right) and by subordinates (not wanting to upset the boss). Equally, we often bring negative prejudices to our assessments, such as anecdotal and glibly made judgements that can cloud our sense of what actually is happening. 'He's always been a poor kick', 'She always does that', 'He never gets the ball when the opposition mark him' and the like are all telltale signs of such folly from those whose greatest capacity should be to make objective, reasoned assessments of performance.

This is why accurate, impartial and sufficient statistics are so important in 'reality-testing' our assertions and judgements. The best coaches and managers will pay heed to the messages contained in a statistical appraisal of performance.

It was no less so in Shakespeare's time – or indeed, if Shakespeare can be believed historically, in the time of Julius Caesar:

**But men may construe things after their
fashion,
Clean from the purpose of the things
themselves**

Julius Caesar, I.iii, lines 34–35

Here, Cicero is less than impressed by Casca's assertion that there are ominous portents afoot. Similarly, the modern-day leader will

ensure that statistics are accurate, appropriate and unambiguous.

Shakespeare also has something to say
about dealing with loss and being able to
recover our composure so that we act with
utility – another important lesson in objectivity. Excessive emotion in either direction can
be distracting and inefficient. Lafeu, an old
and sentimental lord, comments about the
need for moderation and the dangers of excess:

Moderate lamentation is the right of the dead:
Excessive grief the enemy of the living

All's Well That Ends Well, I.i, lines 48–49

Finally, it is necessary for us to know what we
can fix and what we cannot. Lady Macbeth
suggests to her husband that he should know
this now that their murderous plotting is
afoot. What they have set in motion cannot
be changed:

. . . Things without all remedy
Should be without regard. What's done is
done

Macbeth, III.ii, lines 11–12

Coaching lesson

To avoid the error of selective abstraction, and to always lead with true objectivity, there are a number of precautions that will serve you well. Firstly, make sure you have high quality statistical data that will either support or contradict your impression. Listen to others . . . trusted lieutenants must be willing to disagree and have their own views . . . otherwise they are redundant! Seek the view of others in the game. Nobody knows better than the other team in a contest how much a player hurts them! *Never* say *never*; over time performances change and last year's struggler can become this year's champion. Take a long-term view as a patch of poor performance may not reflect lack of capacity. The instances in sport and business are too numerous to outline the truth of this. Keep an open mind!

CHAPTER 9

PATIENCE

How poor they are that have not patience!
What wound did ever heal but by degrees?

Othello, II.iii, lines 358–359

Iago is plotting the downfall of Othello and using Roderigo, a gullible Venetian gentleman who also fancies Othello's wife, to cause strife. Roderigo is frustrated with the lack of progress but is here cautioned by Iago to be patient. The subterfuge will take *time* . . .

Great enterprises take time to plan and build, and similarly great teams and athletes are nurtured carefully in their evolution. The capacity to be patient and persistent is essential in the armoury of coaches and athletes alike.

Persistence is tied up with the will and

determination to keep going. It ignites our internal engine to keep us working to achieve our goals. However, persistence can be blind and pointless if it is not backed up by wise thought, planning, preparation and flexibility. This is the cerebral part of the equation, where the mind is at the centre of the action. Patience is the wisdom behind smart persistence. It is tied up in the mind's ability to see your way through a problem. It is necessary if we are to achieve worthwhile goals and it reinforces our resilience sometimes when things might go wrong.

Hence, Iago continues to Roderigo, the smart thing to do is allow time to pass:

Thou know'st we work by wit, and not by witchcraft;
And wit depends on dilatory time

[dilatory = the passing of]
Othello, II.iii, lines 360–361

Shakespeare makes this point throughout his works. In *Henry V*, for instance, Corporal Nim is plotting and scheming with Lieutenant Bardolph but recognises the necessity for patience in their deviant dealings:

. . . though patience be a tired mare, yet she
will plod . . .

Henry V, II.i, lines 23–24

Essential to learning

An essential element in achieving success is the
ability to build up your program by learning
new skills and changing bad habits and practices that are not efficient. This entails
'relearning' and 'over-learning', and sometimes
requires stripping bare what is already in
place. This can never be rushed and often
requires regression before progress can be
made. Just as making adjustments to one's golf
swing or technique and any such skill –
whether it be hitting, kicking, throwing or running – requires time, patience and persistence.

Shakespeare's Friar Laurence felt similarly
about the course of love as an antidote for the
rancour that existed between the Capulets
and the Montagues in *Romeo and Juliet*. In
one scene Romeo emerges from a blissful
evening with Juliet and reveals his intentions
to the good Friar; perhaps a liaison could join
the households in a happy way, muses Laurence. The young Montague is impatient but
Friar Laurence cautions:

Wisely and slow, they stumble that run fast

Romeo and Juliet, II.iii, line 94

Quality practices require patience in their learning and perfecting – Shakespeare as a golf professional would have given the same message that the good Friar used to caution Romeo. (And Romeo would have been wise to take it!) Nick Faldo spent more than a year reconstructing his golf swing with telling effect in the 1980s.

Alas, Romeo was not listening. After he kills Tybalt, Juliet's cousin, he is banished from Verona. For Romeo, death would be a better punishment if he cannot be with Juliet. Friar Laurence again offers sage advice to Romeo, which we know of course he won't take:

Be patient, for the world is broad and wide

Romeo and Juliet, III.iii, line 16

Patience means breaking the task into manageable bits. It is by paying attention to each small part of a task that the big picture falls into place and great deeds are done. Such messages aren't 'sexy' or 'fashionable' yet they hold true over time. The Bard clearly was aware of that:

And many strokes, though with a little axe
Hews down and fells the hardest – timbered
oak

Henry VI, II.iii, lines 54–55

Patient, but never passive

All of this is well and good but a common mistake that coaches make in the contest is to tell their players to 'be patient' when putting in place their game plan. Often 'be patient' is construed by athletes as a request to be 'passive' rather than proactive. Nothing could be more fatal or undesirable because passivity takes the edge off sharpness and dynamism, and that is never the intention.

What the coach really wants is athletes making the plan work, not waiting to see what happens. Any business would say the same of its plans and strategies: don't wait to see how it turns out – get on with it. Shakespeare's evil Iago certainly knew this. He didn't just wait to see Othello fall, he was actively and constantly engineering it!

There is often a quick and easy way or

short cut but the 'wisely and slow' method of Friar Laurence will usually bring great rewards. Patience is about being able to defer or delay gratification – a lesson learnt hopefully by every child in the formative years. The alternative is a frightening rush to fulfil one's desire without consideration for long-term outcomes or short-term consequences.

In *The Rape of Lucrece*, Shakespeare outlines the dangers of such folly:

What win I if I gain the thing I seek?
A dream, a breath, a froth of fleeting joy.
Who buys a minute's mirth to wail a week?
Or sells eternity to get a toy?
For one sweet grape who will the vine
    destroy?

The Rape of Lucrece, lines 211–215

The message is clear. Plan for the long term; don't get lost seeking quick, easy, short-term rewards.

Coaching lesson

Patience is the quality of mind that allows you to see your plans through to their conclusion. Along the way, assimilating new knowledge and new skills, techniques and ideas can be time consuming, but impatience can easily create anxiety and tension that militate against ideal learning.

Of course, it is a necessity to be vigilant and aggressive about making progress. Patience is not incompatible with this vigilance. It just reminds us that in seeing something through to its conclusion, sometimes we will stumble.

CHAPTER 10

PRAISE AND COURAGE

Praise

Praise us as we are tasted, allow us as we prove ...

Troilus and Cressida, III.ii, lines 87–88

Here, Troilus is asking Cressida to treat him as she finds him. He will show how faithful he can be. (Not that she proves so reliable herself, of course!)

Coaches do three things when preparing and training their athletes: praise, redirect and reprimand. While positive reinforcement is most enjoyed by those in the team, all three have their place. This is indeed what any employee or athlete ought to receive and expect from their manager or coach.

What is crucial in your organisation is that you be consistent in your treatment of your charges. Appropriate reward and recognition of good performance is crucial to build confidence, trust and belief. Also, however appropriate, redirection and sometimes reprimand should accompany poor performance. The crucial element of this process is that criticism should be constructive, offer solutions and also provide support for the remedy, whatever that may be.

'Tis not enough to help the feeble up,
But to support him after . . .

Timon of Athens, I.i, lines 110–111

While Timon is generous in supporting those he thinks are his friends, he finds himself used by them and eventually in penury. However, the sentiment expressed is sound, as Timon's friend Ventidius is in need of help having been imprisoned over his debt. Timon will pay it out and then help him get back on his feet. (Unfortunately for him, Timon's many friends prove to be of the 'fair weather' variety when he himself is in need of assistance!)

As stated previously, the best coaching environments offer support and advice. Those who have not achieved their goals or attained the appropriate level of competence require attention and vigilance. Even the greatest need this. The best technical and tactical athletes in my teams needed continual prodding and guidance to attain their physical potential, and only through this were they able to exhibit their skills to the greatest extent. Similarly, there will be times when every individual is beset with problems outside that can militate against high performance. Support is critical at such times.

All of us seek approval in our endeavours. We are rewarded in various ways; some tangible (money, position, status), some intangible (self-satisfaction, self-esteem, praise and belonging). The best coaches always praise and reward good performance with immediate approval and encouragement.

One good deed dying tongueless
Slaughters a thousand waiting upon that.
Our praises are our wages; you may ride's
With one soft kiss a thousand furlongs ere
With spur we heat an acre . . .

The Winter's Tale, I.ii, lines 92–96

Hermione is making a case here for praise as a motivator and agent of action. She suggests that the 'carrot' rather than the 'stick' approach is the best way to induce others to perform, and that the effects of withholding praise and reward can be very unproductive. The comparison of the 'soft kiss' versus the 'spur' for the horse is convincing.

Of course the Bard is merely conforming with the sound coaching practice of rewarding good performance with praise and acclamation, wherever or whenever it occurs.

Courage

He's truly valiant that can wisely suffer
The worst that man can breathe,
And make his wrongs his outsides,
To wear them like his raiment carelessly,

[raiment = coat]

And ne'er prefer his injuries to his heart,
To bring it into danger

Timon of Athens, III.v, lines 31–35

True courage, according to the good senator is about the capacity to turn the other cheek. To have belief in oneself and the ability to overcome disappointment and distress is the sort of virtue that is the stuff of champions.

Most of us think immediately of the physical courage required to face mortal danger when we consider this virtue of courage: courage under fire in war or in some natural catastrophe like an earthquake or fire; or courage in risking one's life to save another. We read about such instances all too frequently. Athletes often require physical courage in their sports. Gridiron players, boxers, yachtsmen, a batsman in cricket facing fast bowling at more than 150 kilometres an hour, racing drivers, horse riders, ice hockey players, cyclists or even marathon runners display physical courage. It reflects a capacity, knowing the risks, to put oneself in a position of danger.

However, there is another type of courage displayed by individuals every day. The willingness of athletes to put themselves in positions and places that they fear and are uncomfortable reflects this. To face the prospect of failure, criticism, disappointment and public disapproval takes courage and bravery of a not so overt and visible kind.

Athletes at the highest level face the spectre of public assessment and measurement on a regular basis. It is one of the greatest stressors they face, along with that of being required to continually test themselves in competitive situations in which failure and loss can be swift and painful. Thus courage in all its forms is an appropriate description for athletic performance. It is an indispensable component of the make-up of a champion.

> . . . It is held
> That valour is the chiefest virtue and
> Most dignifies the haver . . .
>
> *Coriolanus*, II.ii. 81–83

In this quotation, Cominius is talking about the status of Coriolanus, who has won a great victory for Rome against the Volscians. He is their greatest warrior and general; the embodiment of courage.

Whatever the situation and the issues faced, all of us must face up to the stresses of uncertainty and fear that require a courageous response.

Coaching lesson

Courage is required for elite athletic performance, and it is not always that of physical bravery. Indeed, that is only a small part of it. Mostly, it is the willingness to commit to situations where you may not succeed yet you are willing to be tested, not knowing what the outcome may be. Praise is a crucial reinforcer for the coach and manager. In preparation, practice and performance it helps sustain confidence and endeavour while reinforcing good practices. While courage sometimes requires physical bravery it is mostly about a willingness to have a go and be tested, in spite of having the odds stacked against you.

In this way, as with so many themes throughout this book, praise and courage are as relevant to the workplace and everyday life as it is to the sporting arena or the battlefield triumphs described in a number of Shakespeare's plays.

CHAPTER 11

PREPARATION

It is most meet we arm us 'gainst the foe;
For peace itself should not so dull a
    kingdom,
Though war nor no known quarrel were in
    question,
But that defences, musters, preparations,
Should be maintain'd assembled, and
    collected,
As were a war in expectation

Henry V, II.iv, lines 15–20

The Dauphin (as the son and heir to the throne of France was known) agrees with his father that it is right to be prepared but he foolishly underestimates a Henry V reborn from his frivolous youth. This error coupled with poor preparation leads to a crushing defeat for the French at Agincourt.

This piece, especially the last three lines, had a resonance for the Europe of the late 1930s. There is no substitute for being prepared and ready. The great contests of Shakespeare's days were on the battlefield not at the Olympic Games or Wembley Stadium or Twickenham, but of course the analogies hold firm for a modern sporting and commercial world just as they do today for world geo-politics.

All things are ready, if our minds be so

Henry V, IV.iii, line 71

On the other side of the battle, Henry remarks on the readiness of his men to fight the French at Agincourt. This comment comes after his famous 'band of brothers' speech.

Good preparation is what gives confidence and belief when we set out on an enterprise. Can you remember the trepidation you felt before that algebra exam when you hadn't done your exercises or homework for the term? Knowing that you'd dealt with the problems before and had a track record of doing the work would've been the only thing that could have given you confidence – unless of course you managed to get hold of a copy of the paper and solutions the day before!

Shakespeare is correct to see it as a state of mind and a discipline with urgency, for these are crucial elements of being prepared. If you want to cut corners or leave things out, you will pay for them in the contest. If you aren't tuned in, attentive and alert you will miss things that might make a difference.

Often the work of preparing is not easy. It may require drudgery and repetition. In order to make progress in our physical conditioning we need to overload our physiological system in order to get adaptation and progression. This often entails many thankless hours of unseen and exhausting work.

After her third grand slam victory, in Melbourne in 2004, Justine Henin-Hardenne talked about her decision to go back to the work of serious training off-season. The decision was made soon after her win at the US Open many months earlier. 'It wasn't easy to go back to work like that again; I admit it. It wasn't that obvious to get re-motivated, but Pat [her fitness trainer] was there to push me from the first day. He put me back to work, and you know, he has always said to me, "You will remember all this when you lift the trophy." And every time I lift a trophy, I do think about it.'

Vigilance

. . . I am as vigilant as a cat to steal cream

Henry IV, Part I, IV.ii, lines 56–57

Without attention to the details any enterprise will fail. If I have had a theme or motto for my time as a coach, it must surely have been that 'The price of life is eternal vigilance'. Considering the options, preparing for the possibilities, scouting the opposition, ensuring thoroughness in all your processes and plans, ensures that you are seldom surprised. As with the pursuit of excellence discussed earlier, it ensures that you have responses on hand to deal with difficult problems.

Vigilance is essential because of the folly of complacency, which is the state of mind that most corrupts successful businesses and teams. Shakespeare would not have allowed his team to fall into that trap:

The path is smooth that leadeth on to danger

Venus and Adonis, line 788

Shakespeare warns about the course of love that 'never runs true' but whatever the enterprise, a good rule of thumb is to be even more vigilant when things appear to be running *smoothly*.

It is not the stuff of the young usually, nor of glamorous celebration or fame. It does not get much coverage in the media and it isn't the 'Gucci' part of coaching but vigilance gives you a quality preparation and the development of good habits that serve one well under pressure or when pressed to perform. It keeps you awake, sharpens your defences and ensures that no stone is left unturned.

On meeting Romeo, Friar Laurence quickly assesses that he has been up all night. Laurence displays the sort of acuity and alertness that notices things, that reads the signs. Vigilance is not necessarily a thing of youth. You most usually find it in a trained, disciplined observer, and the good Friar is such a person.

**Care keeps his watch in every old man's eye,
And where care lodges sleep will never lie**

Romeo and Juliet, II.iii, lines 35–36

Similarly, honing old skills and developing and perfecting new ones requires much repetition and many hours of challenging work. It has always been that way, as it was in Shakespeare's time.

The great 'readiness' quote in Shakespeare comes in *Hamlet*, in which the Prince takes a fatalistic approach to impending events. The final meeting with Claudius and his death (indeed, many deaths) is ahead; Horatio suggests Hamlet might like to avoid the situation, but Hamlet is ready:

**Not a whit, we defy augury: there is a
    special**   [augury = speculation, fortune telling]
**providence in the fall of a sparrow. If it be
    now, 'tis not to come; if it be not to
    come, it will be now, if it be not now, yet
    it will come – the readiness is all . . .**

Hamlet, V.ii, lines 211–215

While such an approach can offer a release of performance pressure, it may also militate against preparing thoroughly as it could encourage the view that it is not in your hands – the outcome is in the hands of a higher power. (I remember in my playing days, I always felt a little envious of the Pakistanis who were able to leave the worrying up to Allah, when those of us without this prop had to assume all care and responsibility ourselves!)

Coaching lesson

As a coach I saw training sessions as the most crucial part of preparation, for they afforded the opportunity to mimic the match. I always endeavoured to create realistic situations that were physically and mentally more taxing than the game.

Without planned, appropriate, diligent preparation, we can never feel we are confident and ready to compete. The most important thing coaches do is to conceptualise, organise and supervise the preparation.

Chapter 12

RESILIENCE

Sweet are the uses of adversity
> *As You Like It*, II.i, line 12

While the Duke Senior is living in banishment in the forest of Arden, he muses about how life without the trappings and comforts of the court has many other advantages.

Perhaps the greatest test to leadership comes when one faces disappointment, failure or adversity. Whatever the endeavour, you can be sure that things will go wrong at some stage, and it is our capacity to face adversity, overcome it and continue performing – which is the real test of the organisation or team.

Time and again Shakespeare makes this

point, which is why it is a theme that echoes throughout this book. He does it in many different ways. In one of his sonnets, for example, he makes the point that familiarity can breed contempt:

And sweets grown common lose their dear delight

Sonnet 102, line 12

Scarcity is good sometimes as it sharpens our appreciation of what we have or had, and stirs our desire to have more of it!

Perhaps my favourite quote on this topic comes from *Cymbeline*. A forthright Innogen (Imogen) puts it so well as, lost, she enters a cave not knowing what is ahead:

Plenty and peace breeds cowards; hardness ever
Of hardiness is mother . . .

Cymbeline, III.vi, lines 21–22

Toughness is the outcome of experiencing difficult times and enduring. If all things go well, we are in danger of becoming soft and complacent, and unable to deal with difficulties when they arise.

The best teams, organisations or businesses are resilient in that they prevail over adversity. They are analytical about their weaknesses, face up to their problems and persist in the face of difficulties. In *Henry VI, Part III*, Queen Margaret, bravely facing up to what looks like a lost cause, entreats her followers with these words:

. . . wise men ne'er sit and wail their loss,
But cheerly seek how to redress their harms

Henry VI, Part III, V.iv, lines 1–2

Unfortunately for Margaret, she's backed the wrong horse and does not have long left on this earth! However, her sentiment in face of mortal peril is admirable.

Few of us in modern life would find ourselves in such a position but we all have to overcome setbacks. In sporting contests a loss does not need to mean that all is lost. In the football World Cup of 1994, Italy lost their first match but had the resilience to regroup and ended up playing in the final many weeks later. As mentioned in the Introduction, the

French team, champions all, were not able to turn around their fortunes in 2002 after a similar beginning.

Truly resilient people and teams base their hopes on their ability to face up to the harsh realities of their present situation and put in place a strategy to overcome the present problems, difficulties and threats. They 'seek to redress their harms' not with blind hope but with calculated analytical action and effort. The great gift of experience on your team is to have people who have been there before and who know that there is a way through present problems. Indeed, this is a cornerstone of great leadership.

Luck/chance

Those that are truly resilient will handle 'the slings and arrows of outrageous fortune' to which Hamlet most famously referred. Sometimes we are all faced with lucky or unlucky events. The test of our resilience is in the response to such events that, by their nature, are outside our control.

Nestor, a Greek commander, in discussion with the Greek general Agamemnon and other commanders, makes the point that the true test of men lies in the way they cope with chance:

... In the reproof of chance
Lies the true proof of men ...

Troilus and Cressida, I.iii, lines 33–34

The aim of the coach is to deal will all the things that can come along; expected and unexpected (or even bizarre) events. As stated elsewhere, you must have strategies prepared to cope with such events. There is little one can do about some things or the good or bad fortune that is difficult to predict or prepare for. Athletes must understand that they cannot allow such events to disturb their focus on the task. In the sporting context the sudden injury, freakish brilliance of an opponent, unusual weather or pitch conditions or questionable umpiring decision all come into this category. Yet to be successful and consistent, one must be able to cope. To expect the unexpected and deal with it is the requirement.

Again, my strategy for preparing for such eventualities is to overload training and preparation with decisions, to make it harder and more complex than the game itself in order to build resilient athletes capable of taking the worst misfortune in their stride without losing focus or their goal. Like it or not, life, business and sport all entertain an element of chance. The skilled practitioner knows when to seize such events as opportunity. Timing and a willingness to back oneself are thus crucial for the successful performer.

Brutus outlines to Cassius the need to act when the conditions are most advantageous – to utilise the opportunity to strike – as 'the enemy increaseth every day':

There is a tide in the affairs of men
Which, taken at the flood, leads on to
**   fortune;**
Omitted, all the voyage of their life
Is bound in shallows and in miseries

Julius Caesar, IV.iii, lines 216–219

'Seize the day', as the motto goes!

A fatalistic approach to performance and success can be soothing and reassuring but should we abandon our fate to the gods? While Shakespeare acknowledges the existence of serendipity, Pisanio, the servant of

Posthumus, muses over events out of his control and which cannot be known:

Fortune brings in some boats that are not steer'd

Cymbeline, IV.iii, line 46

Those who wait to see the outcome and a solution are not the ones you want on your team. While sometimes fortune may favour you, the best and most resilient make their way in spite of good or bad luck. They become that way by seeing opportunity in adversity and 'cheerly seek how to address their harms'.

Loss

Finally, something ought to be said about loss and disappointment, a subject that we've touched on elsewhere. The experience and overcoming of losses are ever present in the sporting landscape and crucial formative events in all athletes. 'Losing to win', while seeming paradoxical, is often the pathway to ultimate triumphs. Many of the England team that raised the William Webb Ellis Cup at the Sydney Olympic Stadium in November 2003 had been disappointed losers in the quarter finals four years earlier.

The most stressful loss experience faced in everyday life is the loss of a loved one. It invokes reactions of denial and isolation, anger, bargaining to regain control, depression characterised by sadness and hopelessness, and finally acceptance – whereby feelings, while still deeply felt, do not overwhelm. These same emotions accompany losing a connection with important facets of our lives. Being disconnected or losing touch with people, objects, valued experiences or even some aspect of self-esteem or self-awareness will provoke these responses.

Grieving is a process through which we all pass at different stages of our lives. The athlete suffers injury, loss of form, selection disappointments and retirement issues, all of which carry the burden of loss and distress. In business, ups and downs are equally inevitable. The really resilient overcome these setbacks and find a way forward for there comes a time when we must move on. Every champion knows that.

In one of Shakespeare's last plays, *The Winter's Tale*, he reminds us of this:

... What's gone and what's past help
Should be past grief ...

The Winter's Tale, III.ii, lines 221–222

Coaching lesson

Perhaps the most outstanding contemporary sports example of great resilience is the story of an aspiring Olympic cyclist struck down by what appeared to be a fatal disseminated cancer. In 1996 Lance Armstrong faced an illness that would strip away his ambitions and dreams, and most likely his life. Now the winner of five consecutive Tour de France races, Armstrong is aiming for an unprecedented sixth victory. Adversity, scarcity, bad luck, unexpected events, disappointments and losses all make the resilient even more determined to succeed. Resilient individuals and groups face up to the reality that confronts them. They analyse it, find solutions and set about putting their solutions into practice.

Chapter 13

RESOURCEFULNESS

> ... A good wit will make use of anything.
> I will turn diseases to commodity
>
> *Henry IV, Part II*, I.ii, lines 246–247

A jestering Falstaff is trying to see or find the good in being plagued by gout or pox – perhaps both.

The coaching lesson here is one of the most important. It has to do with being resilient and optimistic and most of all pragmatic. You have to have the capacity to make do with what you have, conjure up solutions, find new ways and utilise the available capacity.

Not everyone coaches Manchester United and can have any player they want. The resourceful coach takes the position that no matter what, he or she will make the best of it. Often this means turning perceived difficulties and obstacles into advantages, and when things go wrong focusing on fixing things not blaming or lamenting.

It is seldom the case that things go easily so it is important that we are able to find solutions, solve problems and overcome setbacks by being resourceful. Shakespeare understood that the world was a difficult place and through Rosalind's eyes it seems so:

O, how full of briers is this working-day world!

As You Like It, I.iii, line 12

The Bard also knew that sometimes you have to choose from some not so attractive option:

. . . there's small choice in rotten apples

The Taming of the Shrew, I.i, line 130

To be resourceful requires the pragmatism to try things. Perhaps the greatest danger to your team or organisation is to be too risk-averse, too fearful or too worried about making mistakes. Any enterprise requires a balance between silly risk and being a 100 per cent sure before acting. 'Calculated risks' are the stuff of brave discovery and action.

In *Cymbeline*, Giacomo is trying to summon up the courage to seduce Imogen in order to win his bet with Lionatus, her husband, who proclaims her fidelity. The context may be frivolous but the message is valid:

. . . Boldness be my friend!
Arm me, audacity, from head to foot!

Cymbeline, I.vi, lines 18–19

The resourceful coach decides what is needed and is willing to back his or her judgement and act. This entails being decisive, acting when necessary, facing up to problems that exist, and dealing with them in spite of how unpleasant that might be.

King Henry, while old and unwell, is still keen to marshal his resources:

Are these things then necessities?
Then let us meet them like necessities

Henry IV, Part II, III.i, lines 92–93

The resourceful, therefore, make virtue of necessity. Indeed this phrase, part of our everyday language now, is a 'Shakespearism'. He used the words in a number of places. In Richard II, John Gaunt suggests to his son Bolingbroke, the future Henry IV, that he make his banishment work for him; he suggests there is '. . . no virtue like necessity . . .'

Circumstances beyond our control often give us no options other than our own resourcefulness, inventiveness and flexibility. Being resourceful is essentially about 'making virtue of necessity'.

The resourceful often surprise and exceed what is expected. They make something out of nothing, and find solutions and means unpredictable and novel. That is their great strength.

> . . . doing, in the figure of a lamb, the feats of a lion . . .
>
> *Much Ado About Nothing*, I.i, line 14–15

Recently on the BBC I saw a reporter suggest that new evidence opened the door on some matter sufficiently for the investigation to gain momentum. He quoted the Bard:

No 'tis not so deep as a well, nor so wide as
    a church door; but 'tis enough, 'twill
    serve

Romeo and Juliet, III.i, lines 96–97

Mercutio's description of his mortal wound
certainly didn't match the context but the
reporters point was well made. It is a message
for the resourceful. When an opening appears,
an opportunity presents itself, the resourceful
ever vigilant for their chance will take it.

Coaching lesson

Resourcefulness is embodied in resilient,
optimistic yet pragmatic performers. They
get things done, seek solutions and are
persistent and at times audacious and take
opportunities when they appear. Sometimes
the choices aren't ideal yet they will usually
come up with answers and a way of doing
well beyond expectations. Your team or
organisation can never have enough
resourceful individuals.

CHAPTER 14

SELF-AWARENESS

Greatness knows itself . . .

Henry IV, Part I, IV.iii, line 76

A fool doth think he is wise, but the wise man knows himself to be a fool

As You Like It, V.i, line 31

These two quotations appear to be paradoxical statements but what they are touching on is the need for true insight and reflection. Socrates' famous quote 'know thyself' was chiselled into the wall of the arts department at my university. It has always stayed with me.

Another famous quote, of course, comes in Shakespeare's most celebrated work –

Hamlet. The oily Polonius offers advice to his son Laertes, who is going away:

This above all – to thine own self be true,
And it must follow, as the night the day,
Thou canst not then be false to any man

Hamlet, I.iii, lines 78–80

Many suggest that this quote promotes greed and selfishness, yet a more sympathetic interpretation is that it can be an appeal to honesty without excluding empathy. Being introspective and analytical about motives and purpose isn't necessarily a formula for only thinking of oneself!

Few of us can fulfil our destiny or realise our potential without knowing ourselves well, without an intimate sense of our own capacities and motivations. Polonius's interpretation could be that by knowing your own inner drives you can truly know your purpose. The art is then to achieve your aim while living in a complex, cooperative social environment.

Self-awareness is a difficult concept for many of us. It entails really coming to grips with where we are and what we are about but, more importantly, being aware of our feelings and thoughts and motivations. It also demands accurate awareness of how our actions affect others. But it is not a passive discovery; it is a dynamic process subject to revision and change. Only by setting out on the journey are we likely to be rewarded and find our inner drives.

Most would say that Polonius's assertion that you cannot 'be false to any man' may appear extreme; but the point about being true to yourself bears our consideration, for it is the centre of all that drives us.

Truly fine performances and the capacity to focus come from self-awareness. The best athletes know themselves well. They understand their strengths and their vulnerabilities, and are able to take advantage of the former and minimise the impact of the latter.

They are able to be candid with themselves about their performances, their training, their preparation and their mental state. The fool overestimates himself, underestimates his opponents and accordingly cuts corners in preparation and 'readiness'. The wise competitor considers all the possible options and rehearses the battle through the eyes of his or her opponent in order to be ready for the unforeseen or unusual.

As has already been outlined, the humility to seek to be better is born in a true assessment of capabilities physical, technical, tactical, mental and cooperative (team orientation). Only by knowing yourself fully do you give yourself the best chance of success. Surely it is the same for any business. The best of them know themselves inside out and are thus able to compete, maximising strengths, minimising weaknesses and recognising and dealing with threats.

As outlined earlier we are often blind to our own faults:

Men's faults do seldom to themselves appear

The Rape of Lucrece, line 633

Shakespeare also makes the point often that in order to truly realise our potential we must take responsibility for what we do. As Cassius says to Brutus when they are plotting the bringing down of the peacock Caesar:

Men at some time are masters of their fates:
The fault, dear Brutus, is not in our stars,
But in ourselves . . .

Julius Caesar, I.ii, lines 139–141

Empathy

The final dividend of 'knowing yourself' is that such insight enhances our own ability to *empathise* with others. This is one of the great bonuses of self-awareness, for our capacity to put ourselves in the shoes of others informs us splendidly of how we ought to behave ourselves.

Shakespeare covers this as well:

... be to yourself
As you would to your friend

Henry VIII, I.i, lines 135–136

Norfolk's advice here to Buckingham in the face of false accusations does not save him but it is nevertheless sound. Empathy enhances the quality of our interactions with others and our capacity to communicate and work cooperatively. Coaches and managers are looking for individuals who value these things and who practise what they know. Such emotional quality can be the glue that holds your team or organisation together.

Reputation

Those who know themselves best have the ability to see themselves accurately in spite of the 'image' the world may hold of them. Reputation is contingent on the view of others; often it is the antithesis of self-awareness.

> . . . Reputation is an idle and most false imposition; oft got without merit, and lost without deserving
>
> *Othello*, II.iii, lines 259–260

Here, Iago is trying to reassure Cassio that reputation isn't all. (The latter, a loyal lieutenant, has just been dismissed by his general, Othello, for being involved in a brawl, which Iago has engineered!) Cassio bemoans his loss of reputation but ironically Iago, the really evil and envious lieutenant, while proclaiming himself an 'honest man', decries the worth of reputation!

Shakespeare seeks to highlight the difference between appearance and reality. In the course of this play the word 'honest' is used to refer to Iago many times, yet he is one of Shakespeare's most evil villains. Reputation can be a useful guide to worth but equally it can deceive. Again in Antony's famous speech after Caesar's murder, he uses the same ploy: Brutus and Cassius are portrayed as 'honourable men'.

Many, of course, are happy to believe their reputation rather than to ask themselves the hard questions or seek solutions from within. Lear avoids the truth about himself in a tragedy of epic proportions, until he eventually asks the question:

Who is it that can tell me who I am?

King Lear, I.iv, line 229

But it is left to the Fool to answer: 'Lear's shadow' – meaning his conscience or the voice within. Lear largely remains oblivious and completely lacking in self-awareness.

Coaches and managers must be ever vigilant when hiring and firing on reputation, yet so often we see mistakes made in these decisions. Clearly, it was no less an issue in Shakespeare's day, when outward appearances and rank assumed even greater importance than they do today.

To build a successful team in your organisation, it is performance that counts; past history and reputation are things that require our attention but also often our scepticism. The ageing champion ought to be viewed with scepticism when seeking to renew for a long term or asking for more money. Extra-ordinarily, in many professional sporting situations, the most productive years are often not the years when the highest remuneration is received. One can understand why players seek security over 'performance pay' yet this very situation militates against better performance as athletes can too easily become complacent and lose the 'edge' that made them great.

Shakespeare knew well the fickle nature of success, power and reputation. In *Cymbeline*, Guiderius sings after he has successfully defeated and beheaded Cloten, the Queen's son, in a fight:

Fear no more the heat o' th' sun
Nor the furious winter's rages;
Thou thy worldly task hast done,
Home art gone, and ta'en thy wages.
Golden girls and lads all must,
As chimney-sweepers, come to dust

Cymbeline, IV.ii, lines 259–263

The best know that they are vulnerable, understand their failings and by working on them, aim to be better. The past record is only a guide to future performance. For coaches, 'current form' has always been the best guide to near-future performance, and the athletes that truly know themselves are your most reliable. They are not always those of highest repute.

This is the dilemma of reputation that we all must be wary of. The past only gives indication of past efforts and not of promise and what will occur or can be achieved.

Coaching lesson

Too often we see champions falter and great teams collapse because they lacked the capacity to truly assess themselves and continue to grow. Honesty with oneself is an indispensable commodity in ensuring this doesn't happen to your organisation, players or team. It is also important to improve our ability to relate to others and communicate our aims and ideas effectively.

CHAPTER 15

STRATEGY AND TACTICS

... and the devil hath power
T' assume a pleasing shape ...

Hamlet, II.ii, lines 595–596

Till then 'tis wisdom to conceal our meaning

Henry VI, Part III, IV.vii, line 60

The essence of strategy (and strategy is central to the success of any enterprise) is the ability to surprise an opponent, to be underestimated, to be better prepared or to be quickly able to adapt to changes, be they good or bad.

'Appearances can be deceptive.' Hamlet knows this and, in the first of the quotations above, is concerned that the ghost he has seen may be the devil in disguise. In the line from *Henry VI, Part III*, Edward IV, soon to reclaim the throne for the House of York, wants time for his forces to grow stronger and sees value in hiding their intentions.

Of course, deception is the central core of strategy. It is best to appear as you are not: if you are slow, try to appear fast; if flexible, appear rigid; if light, appear heavy; if hard, appear soft. Such is the essence of deception and the cornerstone of strategy.

Even a fool knows that there is value in disguising your capabilities. In *King Lear* the Fool plays the role of teaching Lear the extent of his foolishness and underlining the message that appearance can deceive:

Have more than thou showest,
Speak less than thou knowest,
Lend less than thou owest,
Ride more than thou goest,
Learn more than thou trowest,

[trow = believe, think, know]

Set less than thou throwest

King Lear, I.iv, lines 117–122

Hardly 'foolish' advice, the role of 'the Fool' in Lear is that of a muse who reflects and underlines the magnitude of the King's folly. Unfortunately, Lear, without plausible strategy, too proud, easily duped and misguided, is unable to take the Fool's advice.

There are, of course, some other important aspects of strategy, and Shakespeare it seems was in touch with most of them.

Be decisive

It is a mistake to spend too long making up your mind what to do. The right moment for action can be lost if one is not able to be decisive.

A little fire is quickly trodden out,
Which, being suffer'd, rivers cannot quench

Henry VI, Part III, IV.viii, lines 7–8

It is certainly best to deal with a threat when it is most manageable.

Never underestimate your opponent

It is best to always consider the worst-case scenario when assessing the risk of any venture.

In cases of defence, 'tis best to weigh
The enemy more mighty than he seems

Henry V, II.iv, lines 43–44

King Charles VI's son and heir, the Dauphin, warns against underestimating the strength of King Henry's men. In the end the French are defeated by a significantly smaller force. The lesson: there is more to the strength of a force than mere numbers.

Plan carefully

While the need for quick decisive action is always present, one would be foolish to act without first knowing what you plan to achieve and without considering all the possibilities that may beset you on any one day.

In *Henry IV, Part II*, Bardolph uses the analogy of building to outline a strategy to overthrow Henry after the setback at Shrewsbury and the death of Hotspur. Together with Mowbray (the Archbishop of York), Marshal and Hastings, they must 'build' another challenge and in so doing consider whether that is indeed a good idea:

... When we mean to build,
We first survey the plot, then draw the model;
And when we see the figure of the house,
Then must we rate the cost of the erection;
Which if we find outweighs ability,
What do we then but draw anew the model
In fewer offices, or at least desist
To build at all? ...

Henry IV, Part II, I.iii, lines 40–47

Indeed to decide to withdraw because conditions might not be favourable is often appropriate strategy!

Pick your time

Polonius giving advice to his son seeks to make sure that Laertes is never impetuous in his actions:

... Beware
Of entrance to a quarrel; but, being in,
Bear't that th' opposed may beware of thee

Hamlet, I.iii, lines 65–67

Indeed, letting the opposition know your strength can have its place if you intend acting on this. It can have the effect of demoralising or distracting. When you commit then you must do so wholeheartedly. Half measures are seldom successful.

Take advice

Modern management and coaching requires the integration of information from a wide variety of sources, internal and external, expert and pragmatic. The true quality of your strategy and tactics requires the ingestion and digestion of all of this information.

The best coaches know how to listen and will utilise a variety of resources. Polonius thought this message worthy for his departing son Laertes:

Give every man thy ear, but few thy voice;
Take each man's censure, but reserve thy
   judgment

Hamlet, I.iii, lines 68–69

Use power appropriately (avoid excess)

Finally, Shakespeare suggests, through Isabella, the measured use of power and resources as she is pleading for her brother's life:

. . . O, it is excellent
To have a giant's strength!
But it is tyrannous
To use it like a giant

Measure for Measure, II.ii, lines 107–109

Any coach will tell you that there is a time to be dominant, assertive and all powerful, and a time to keep your powder dry to fight another day. Too dominant a performance often creates a will and energy in your opponent that will eventually bring you down, whereas a closer contest can create a false sense of worth in an opponent. Knowing yourself and using your resources to last in the long term is prudent strategy.

Coaching lesson

- Never reveal too much for there is value in having something in reserve.
- Be willing to act decisively when your judgement determines it.
- Plan to deal with the worst possibilities and know your enemies well.
- Know when to withdraw to fight another day, and when committed, pick your time to fight.
- Listen to advice; never stop listening but reserve your judgement, and use your power wisely – avoiding excesses.

These points lay down the rudiments of a strategy for competition that are appropriate for your team or business. Shakespeare understood the art of war in much the same manner as the ancient Chinese philosopher Sun Tsu.

CHAPTER 16

TEAMWORK

We few, we happy few, we band of brothers

Henry V, IV.iii, line 60

As an actor, playwright, owner and investor, Shakespeare knew his business well. He understood the need for a group of players to combine together and cooperate in the production of a play. The theatre at that time largely operated on a repertory system, with a considerable variety of plays available and a different one played each afternoon. Shakespeare understood that teamwork was required to succeed in the business, and his success as a businessman reflected that approach. In around 1612 he retired to Stratford-upon-Avon a wealthy man.

Team sport as we know it today was not on the agenda in Elizabethan England but the activity that most identified with cooperative enterprise was the military. The plays are dotted with references to the brotherhood of fighting together for the cause of King and country. These references pertain to our modern sense of teamwork.

In the largest framework, the words of the cynical and irreverent Jacques in the forest of Arden describe how each of us has a role to play on a much larger canvas. This is one of Shakespeare's best known pieces.

All the world's a stage,
And all the men and women merely players;
They have their exits and their entrances;
And one man in his time plays many parts

As You Like It, II.vii, lines 139–142

He goes on to describe the seven ages of man from infant, school boy, lover, soldier, sage justice, old man and, finally, a second childishness before oblivion.

The theme of the harmony of the universe is pursued further in *Troilus and Cressida*, wherein Ulysses famously compares society with a stringed instrument, playing in harmony until that harmony is broken when one of the elements is out of tune, even if only by a small amount:

**Take but degree away, untune that string,
And hark what discord follows! . . .**

Troilus and Cressida, I.iii, lines 109–110

Teamwork requires individuals to perform their roles with thoroughness, trusting that their team-mates will do likewise, and coaches endeavour as much as possible to outline to the whole team the connections and interdependence that makes great teams reliable, productive and efficient. Each part, large or small can be crucial.

Another example of teamwork in one of Shakespeare's works sees Theseus, the Duke of Athens, reflecting on the untimely death of Arcite, which brings good fortune to the other noble kinsman, Palamon:

**His part is played, and though it were too
short, he did it well**

Two Noble Kinsmen, I.iv, line 102

So to the 'band of brothers', outnumbered at least five to one. The English win an improbable victory at Agincourt against the French, who underestimate English resolve. Indeed, Henry's rousing St Crispin's Day speech before the battle plays a part in the victory. Interestingly, the King's quiet time spent with his men the night before battle is given considerable coverage by Shakespeare. The Bard clearly understands the dynamics of leadership in such an enterprise. While the rousing speech gets most of the coverage, the quiet preparation is more important in laying down the resolve behind Henry's win.

The appeal to 'brotherhood' and togetherness in the words and the sense of 'us' conveyed very much defines the emotion of a modern team in sport or business, and the pride that devolves from doing something well together:

We few, we happy few, we band of brothers;
For he today that sheds his blood with me
Shall be my brother; be he ne'er so vile,
This day shall gentle his condition;
And gentlemen in England now a-bed
Shall think themselves accurs'd they were
    not here,

**And hold their manhoods cheap whiles any
    speaks
That fought with us upon Saint Crispin's
    day**

Henry V, IV.iii, lines 60–67

The appeal to ownership of that special bond and of the deeds that day resonates with any group. The best teams trust one another and 'own' the performance. Their trust goes to being able to bear their souls without feeling inhibited or 'revealed' in front of one another.

Teams do not succeed without individuals each performing their tasks successfully. To score a goal, try, touchdown or point usually requires a consecutive sequence of perfect actions or of errors forced on opponents. For this to occur, understanding and trust in your team-mates is required for each component of the action.

Mark Antony, after success on the battlefield against Caesar, praises his men for their individual efforts – the sum of which brought victory. In particular, he describes how each man fought as though Antony's cause was his own. This is what occurs in the best teams and organisations. The individuals own the cause and strategy as though it is their own.

For doughty-handed are you, and have
   fought
Not as you serv'd the cause, but as't had
   been
Each man's like mine . . .

Antony and Cleopatra, IV.viii, lines 5–7

This, of course, pertains to every phase of the game. Defence and attack are equally reliant on one another for avoiding errors; executing skills and forcing errors are equally important.

At the highest level no team ever wins a world championship, Olympics, Superbowl or premiership without a well-balanced game at each end of the park. One only needs to look at the records. England, a traditionally defensive soccer nation, won in 1966 with strength at both ends of the park. Brazil's 2002 World Cup winning team did the job in defence but their attack has always been penetrating. Australia and West Indies cricket teams, which have dominated cricket in recent decades, had it in batting and bowling.

The military equivalent of Shakespeare's time was the brotherhood and training of soldiers fighting side by side in battle. The Duke of York, pretending to the crown of Henry VI, displays this trust for his commanders and men as they are being deployed:

In them I trust, for they are soldiers,
Witty, courteous, liberal, full of spirit

Henry VI, Part III, I.ii, lines 42–43

Shakespeare's world may have been vastly different from that of modern sport and business. But his business acumen as an entrepreneur and the machinations of military life provided him with ample knowledge of the functioning of teams and the requirements for and reliance on teamwork to succeed in any cooperative endeavour.

Coaching lesson

Nothing is more important than the team. Building a successful organisation requires the development of a cooperative, trusting group of team players. For the team to succeed each individual has to be committed to the team's goals and perform their role with pride and thoroughness.

118

CHAPTER 17

YOUTH, AGE AND EXPERIENCE

**The oldest hath borne most; we that are
  young
Shall never see so much nor live so long**

King Lear, V.iii, lines 325–326

Here, Edgar delivers the final two lines of the play and actors leave the stage with a dead march carrying the bodies of Lear and Cordelia. The tragedy of Lear sinks into hopelessness as he dies of a broken heart, having destroyed his family and lost his beloved daughter through his foolish, blind pride. The failure of the ageing King to appreciate the rivalry of his siblings and their more youthful ways and ambitions has wrought great havoc on the family.

Securing the best people for your organ-isation and players for your club or team always requires a balance between youth and all it brings, and experience and what that can offer.

As a coach, one of my central pillars of belief is that you 'ignore youth at your peril'. Youth brings openness, enthusiasm, new ideas, ambition and high emotion. All of these things can add something to the vibrancy of your organisation, but the flip side is vulnerability, uncertainty, inconsistency and unrealistic per-ceptions. It is a double-edged sword, and the skilled coach or manager must work hard to realise the rewards and minimise the costs.

In an early scene in *Henry V*, King Harry (Henry V) has just assumed the throne fol-lowing his father's death and he begins to plot action against the French. The action is dis-cussed with enthusiasm before the Archbishop of Canterbury and the Bishop of Ely, who describes the young King thus:

. . . my thrice-puissant liege

[puissant = strong, powerful]

[liege = sovereign lord]

Is in the very May-morn of his youth,

Ripe for exploits and mighty enterprises

Henry V, I.ii, lines 119–121

Yes, Henry is in his prime, an age when all seems possible and the world is to be conquered. There is, of course, a downside to youth as Shakespeare knew only to well.

For one, judgement can be unrefined. Queen Cleopatra admits as much while musing with one of her attendants, Charmian:

My salad days,
When I was green in judgment . . .

Antony and Cleopatra, I.v, lines 75–76

Equally, youth can be fearless or foolhardy:

He jests at scars that never felt a wound

Romeo and Juliet, II.i, line 43

Such confidence can, of course, work for you or against you. The sense of invulnerability that Romeo refers to is usually more reasoned and tempered by age and the experience of the dangers of sword fighting and battles!

Often, youth is also irreverent, unwilling to follow advice of experience. Managing such attitudes can be exceedingly difficult. Biron puts it well when he muses about the powerful emotions of the young:

Young blood doth not obey an old decree

Love's Labour's Lost, IV.iii, line 212

A good example is the Dauphin heir to the French throne. In his cockiness, he completely underestimates a reformed Henry V, formerly Prince Hal. The Dauphin suggests before Agincourt, that the English are led by a 'vain, giddy, shallow, humorous youth'. Indeed, he refuses to take the advice from other nobles: 'You are too much mistaken in this king.'

Age and experience usually bring improved judgement and better ability to assess risk and probabilities as well as an ability to consider alternatives and dispassionately assess possibilities. However, experience and years in the job may not benefit a slow learner. In the same way those who learn well and keenly often seem experienced beyond their years.

His years but young, but his experience old;
His head unmellowed, but his judgment ripe

The Two Gentlemen of Verona, II.iv, lines 65–66

This is Valentine full of praise for the maturity of his friend Proteus.

Usually, or course, experience and judgement are hard-won commodities that result from learning on the job from both successes and mistakes. It is a priceless commodity when honed fully. Again in *The Two Gentlemen of Verona*, Shakespeare makes this point when Antonio is considering the benefits of sending his son off to court to complete his education:

Experience is by industry achiev'd,
And perfected by the swift course of time

The Two Gentlemen of Verona, I.iii, lines 22–23

Accordingly we have the paradox of youth: full of keenness, energy and ideas but sometimes unable to measure the situation or consider all the options, and too quick to rush in. A balance between the strengths and weaknesses is the pathway of good coaching and management.

Perhaps one of the hardest challenges for any coach is to know when the cost of age and experience, measured in decreasing athletic performance and diminished ambition and purpose, is too great. It is then time to renew and institute change. This process should be a continuous one. While difficult and often stressful, it is essential to maintain balance in your team.

Shakespeare often uses gardening analogies, and one in particular comes to mind when discussing age and renewal:

. . . Superfluous branches
We lop away, that bearing boughs may live

Richard II, III.iv, lines 63–64

Here, the Queen hides within earshot while her gardeners discuss the prospects for her failing husband, Richard II. Richard's days are numbered as sovereign – he is considered a superfluous branch!

Coaching lesson

The life of a company, team or any enterprise or family is one of continual renewal, otherwise it will wither and die. Coaches continually sow new seeds and plants while nurturing and pruning their established ones. Eventually, some become woody and too old and unproductive, and they are replaced by even better, stronger, newer and fresher varieties. The coach's experience in horticulture is continually challenged and developed.

The Works of
William Shakespeare

Introduction

. . . We are such stuff, as dreams are made
   on . . .

The Tempest, IV.i, lines 156–157

It is purpose that makes strong the vow

Troilus and Cressida, V.iii, line 23

For 'tis the mind that makes the body rich

Taming of the Shrew, IV.iii, line 168

What sport shall we devise here in this garden,
to drive away the heavy thought of care?

Richard II, III.iv, lines 1–2

If all the year were playing holidays,
To sport would be as tedious as to work

Henry IV, Part I, I.ii, lines 197–198

Talkers are no good doers . . .

Richard III, I.iii, line 351

A *coach's creed*

They that have power to hurt and will do
    none,
That do not do the thing they most do
    show,
Who, moving others, are themselves as stone,
Unmoved, cold, and to temptation slow –
They rightly do inherit Heaven's graces,
And husband nature's riches from expenses;
They are the lords and owners of their faces,
Others but stewards of their excellence.
The summer's flow'r is to the summer sweet
Though to itself it only live and die;
But if that flow'r with base infection meet,
The basest weed out braves his dignity.
For sweetest things turn sourest by their deeds:
Lilies that fester, smell far worse than weeds

Sonnet 94, lines 1–16

Ten favourite quotes
All these quotes appear elsewhere in the book.

Action

Action is eloquence . . .

Coriolanus, III.ii, line 76

**Thy knee bussing the stones – for in such
   business
Action is eloquence, and the eyes of th'
   ignorant
More learned than the ears . . .**

[bussing = kissing]
Coriolanus, III.ii, lines 75–77

**Be great in act, as you
Have been in thought**

King John, V.i, line 45

**Our hands are full of business. Let's away.
Advantage feeds him fat while men delay**

Henry IV, Part I, III.ii, lines 180–181

**Since things in motion sooner catch the eye
Than what stirs not . . .**

Troilus and Cressida III.iii, lines 183–184

... If ever fearful
To do a thing, where I the issue doubted,
Whereof the execution did cry out,
Against the non-performance, 'twas a fear
Which oft infects the wisest ...

The Winter's Tale, I.ii, lines 258–263

Doubts and Fears

Our doubts are traitors,
And makes us lose the good we oft might win
By fearing to attempt ...

Measure for Measure, I.iv, lines 77–79

... When our actions do not,
Our fears do make us traitors

Macbeth, IV.ii, lines 3–4

But cruel are the times, when we are traitors
And do not know ourselves; when we hold
     rumour
From what we fear, and yet know not what
     we fear

Macbeth, IV.ii, lines 18–20

Thus conscience doth make cowards of us all;
And thus the native hue of resolution
Is sicklied o'er with the pale cast of thought,
And enterprises of great pith and moment,
With this regard their currents turn awry
And lose the name of action . . .

[pith = importance]

Hamlet, III.i, lines 83–88

Excellence

Things done well
And with a care exempt themselves from
    fear;
Things done without example, in their issue
Are to be fear'd . . .

Henry VIII, I.ii, lines 88–91

If to do were as easy to know what were
    good to do,
Chapels had been churches and poor men's
    cottages princes' palaces . . .

The Merchant Of Venice, I.ii, lines 11–12

. . . Our bodies are our gardens, to the
    which our wills are gardeners . . .

Othello, I.iii, lines 320–321

What's in a name? That which we call a rose
By any other word would smell as sweet

> *Romeo and Juliet*, II.i, lines 43–44

To business that we love we rise betime,
and go to 't with delight   [betime = early]

> *Antony and Cleopatra*, IV.iv, lines 20–21

Pleasure and action make the hours seem
short

> *Othello*, II.iii, line 367

Humility

It is the witness still of excellency
To put a strange face on his own perfection

> *Much Ado About Nothing*, II.iii, lines 43–44

It is the witness still of excellency
To put a strange face on his own perfection.
I prey thee sing, and let me woo no more

> *Much Ado About Nothing*, II.iii, lines 42–44

What great ones do, the less will prattle of

> *Twelfth Night*, I.ii, line 33

He that loves to be flattered is worthy o' th'
flatterer

Timon of Athens, I.i, lines 229–230

... But 'tis a common proof
That lowliness is young ambition's ladder,
Where the climber-upward turns his face;
But when he once attains the upmost round,
He then unto the ladder turns his back,
Looks in the clouds, scorning the base
    degrees
By which he did ascend ...

Julius Caesar, II.i, lines 21–27

And then I stole all courtesy from heaven,
And dress'd myself in such humility
That I did pluck allegiance from men's
    hearts,
Loud shouts and salutations from their
    mouths

Henry IV, Part I, III.ii, lines 50–53

Leadership – Purpose and Persuasion

The speciality of rule hath been neglected

Troilus and Cressida, I.iii, line 78

. . . it never yet did hurt
to lay down likelihoods and forms of hope

Henry IV, Part II, I.iii, lines 33–34

. . . that glib and oily art
To speak and purpose not . . .

King Lear, I.i, lines 224–225

. . . We are such stuff dreams are made on . . .

The Tempest, IV.i, lines 156–157

It is the purpose that makes strong the vow,
But vows to every purpose must not hold'

Troilus and Cressida, V.iii, lines 23–24

Life every man holds dear, but the dear man
Holds honour far more precious dear than life

Troilus and Cressida, V.iii, lines 27–28

. . . the better part of valour is discretion;
in which better part I have saved my life

Henry IV, Part I, V.iv, lines 118–120

Friends, Romans, countrymen lend me your
ears;
I come to bury Caesar, not to praise him.
The evil that men do lives after them;

The good is oft interred with their bones;
So let it be with Caesar. The noble Brutus
Hath told you Caesar was ambitious.
If it were so, it was a grievous fault;
And grievously hath Caesar answer'd it.
Here, under leave of Brutus and the rest –
For Brutus is an honourable man;
So are they all, all honourable men –
Come I to speak in Caesar's funeral.
He was my friend, faithful and just to me;
But Brutus says he was ambitious;
And Brutus is an honourable man.
He hath brought many captives home to Rome,
Whose ransoms did the general coffers fill;
Did this in Caesar seem ambitious?
When that the poor have cried, Caesar hath
    wept;
Ambition should be made of sterner stuff.
Yet Brutus says he was ambitious;
And Brutus is an honourable man

Julius Caesar, III.ii, lines 73–94

An honest tale speeds best being plainly told

Richard III, IV.iv, lines 358

... brevity is the soul of wit

Hamlet, II.ii, line 90

The silence often of pure innocence
   persuades when speaking fails
           The Winter's Tale, II.ii, lines 41–42

The skipping King, he ambled up and down
With shallow jesters and rash bavin
   wits,   [bavin = brushwood]
Soon kindled and soon burnt; carded his
   state,   [carded = debased]
Mingled his royalty with cap'ring fools
           Henry IV, Part I, III.ii, lines 60–63

Thus I did keep my person fresh and new
           Henry IV, Part I, III.ii, line 55

Learning and Change

O this learning, what a thing it is!
           The Taming of the Shrew, I.ii, line 156

Men's faults do seldom to themselves
   appear;
Their own transgressions partially they
   smother:
This guilt would seem death-worthy in thy
   brother
           The Rape of Lucrece, lines 633–635

I did never think to marry. I must not seem
　　proud; happy are they that hear their
　　distractions and can put them to mending

Much Ado About Nothing, II.iii, lines 219–220

Our remedies oft in ourselves do lie,
Which we ascribe to heaven . . .

All's Well That Ends Well, I.i, lines 202–203

They say, best men are moulded out of
　　faults;
And, for the most, become much more the
　　better

Measure for Measure, V.i, lines 437–438

Mind Over Matter

. . . Present fears
Are less than horrible imaginings

Macbeth, I.iii, lines 136–137

For 'tis the mind that makes the body rich

The Taming of the Shrew, IV.iii, line 168

Striving to better, oft we mar what's well

King Lear, I.iv, line 347

**Fears make devils of cherabuns; they never
    see truly**   [cherabuns = angels]
> *Troilus and Cressida*, III.ii, lines 66–67

**Is it not strange that desire should so many
    years outlive performance?**
> *Henry IV, Part II*, II.iv, lines 250–251

**. . . for there is nothing either good or bad
    but thinking makes it so.
To me it is a prison**
> *Hamlet*, II.ii, lines 248–250

**. . . They say the owl was a baker's daughter
Lord, we know what we are, but know not
    what we may be . . .**
> *Hamlet*, IV.v, lines 40–42

Objectivity

**Make boot of his distraction, never
    anger**   [boot = bounty, advantage]
Made good guard of itself
> *Antony and Cleopatra*, IV.i, lines 8–9

. . . Give me that man
That is not passion's slave, and I will wear him
In my heart's core, ay, in my heart of heart

Hamlet, III.ii, lines 69–71

What to ourselves in passion we propose,
The passion ending, doth the purpose lose

Hamlet, III.ii, 189–190

But men may construe things after their
    fashion,
Clean from the purpose of the things
    themselves

Julius Caesar, I.iii, lines 34–35

Moderate lamentation is the right of the dead:
Excessive grief the enemy of the living

All's Well That Ends Well, I.i, lines 48–49

. . . Things without all remedy
Should be without regard. What's done is
    done

Macbeth, III.ii, lines 11–12

Patience

How poor they are that have not patience!
What wound did ever heal but by degrees?

Othello, II.iii, lines 358–359

Thou knowest we work by wit, and not by
    witchcraft;
And wit depends in dilatory time

[dilatory = the passing of]

Othello, II.iii, lines 360–361

. . . though patience be a tired mare, yet she
    will plod . . .

Henry V, II.i, lines 23–24

Wisely and slow, they stumble that run fast

Romeo and Juliet, II.iii, line 94

Be patient for the world is broad and wide

Romeo and Juliet, III.iii, line 16

And many strokes, though with a little axe
Hews down and fells the hardest – timbered
    oak

Henry V, II.ii, lines 54–55

What win I if I gain the thing I seek?
A dream, a breath, a froth of fleeting joy.
Who buys a minute's mirth to wail a week?
Or sells eternity to get a toy?
For one sweet grape who will the vine destroy?

The Rape of Lucrece, 211–215

Praise and Courage

Praise us as we are tasted, allow us as we
    prove . . .

Troilus and Cressida, III.ii, lines 87–88

'Tis not enough to help the feeble up,
But to support him after . . .

Timon of Athens, I.i, line, 110–111

One good deed dying tongueless
Slaughters a thousand waiting upon that.
Our praises are our wages; you may ride's
With one soft kiss a thousand furlongs ere
With spur we heat an acre . . .

The Winter's Tale, I.ii, lines 92–96

He's truly valiant that can wisely suffer
The worst that man can breathe,
And make his wrongs his outsides,

To wear them like his raiment carelessly,

[raiment = coat]

And ne'er prefer his injuries to his heart,
To bring it into danger

Timon of Athens, III.iv, lines 31–35

... It is held
That valour is the chiefest virtue and
Most dignifies the haver ...

Coriolanus, II.ii, lines 81–83

Preparation

It is most meet we arm us 'gainst the foe;
For peace itself should not so dull a
    kingdom,
Though war nor no known quarrel were in
    question,
But that defences, musters, preparations,
Should be maintain'd assembled, and
    collected,
As were a war in expectation

Henry V, II.iv, lines 15–20

All things be ready, if our minds be so

Henry V, IV.iii, line 71

Vigilance

I am as vigilant as a cat to steal cream

Henry IV, Part I, IV.ii, lines 56–57

**The path is smooth that leadeth on to
danger**

Venus and Adonis, line 788

**Care keeps his watch in every old man's eye,
And where care lodges sleep will never lie**

Romeo and Juliet, II.iii, lines 35–36

**Not a whit, we defy augury: there is a
special**   [augury = speculation, fortune telling]
**providence in the fall of a sparrow. If it be
now, 'tis not to come; if it be not to
come, it will be now, if it be not now, yet
it will come – the readiness is all . . .**

Hamlet, V.ii, lines 211–215

Resilience

Sweet are the uses of adversity

As You Like It, II.i, line 12

And sweets grown common lose their dear
    delight

                        Sonnet 102, Line 12

Plenty and peace breeds cowards, hardiness
    ever
Of hardiness is mother . . .

                    Cymbeline, III.iv, lines 21–22

. . . wise men ne'er sit and wail their loss,
But cheerly seek how to redress their harms

             Henry VI, Part III, V.iv, lines 1–2

. . . In the reproof of chance
Lies the true proof of man . . .

             Troilus and Cressida, I.iii, lines 33–34

There is a tide in the affairs of men
Which, taken at the flood, leads onto
    fortune;
Omitted, all the voyage of their life
Is bound in shallows and in miseries

             Julius Caesar, IV.ii, lines 216–219

Fortune brings in some boats that are not
    steered

                  Cymbeline, IV.iii, line 46

... What's gone and what's past help should
be past grief ...

The Winter's Tale, III.ii, lines 221–222

Resourcefulness

A good wit will make use of anything.
I will turn diseases into commodity

Henry IV, Part II, I.ii, lines 246–247

O, how full of briers is this working-day world!

As You Like It, I.iii, line 12

... there's small choice in rotten apples

The Taming Of The Shrew, I.i, line 130

... Boldness be my friend!
Arm me, audacity, from head to foot!

Cymbeline, I.vi, lines 18–19

Are these things then necessities?
Then let us meet them like necessities

Henry IV, Part II, III.i, lines 92–93

... doing, in the figure of a lamb, the feats
of a lion ...

Much Ado About Nothing, I.i, line 13

No 'tis so deep as a well, nor so wide as a
    church door; but 'tis enough, 'twill serve

Romeo and Juliet, III.i, lines 96–97

Self-Awareness

Greatness knows itself . . .

Henry IV, Part I, IV.iii, line 76

A fool doth think he is wise,
but the wise man knows himself to be a fool

As You Like It, V.i, line 31

This above all – to thine own self be true,
And it must follow, as the night the day,
Thou canst not then be false to any man

Hamlet, I.iii, lines 78–80

Men's faults do seldom to themselves appear

The Rape of Lucrece, line 633

Men at some time are masters of their fates:
The fault, dear Brutus, is not in our stars,
But in ourselves . . .

Julius Caesar, I.ii, lines 139–141

. . . be to yourself
As you would to your friend . . .

Henry VIII, I.i, lines 135–136

. . . reputation is an idle and most false
imposition; oft got without merit, and lost
without deserving

Othello, I.iii, lines 259–260

Who is it that can tell me who I am?

King Lear, I.iv, line 229

Fear no more the heat o' th' sun,
Nor the furious winter's rages;
Thou thy worldly task hast done,
Home art gone, and ta'en thy wages.
Golden girls and lads all must,
As chimney-sweepers, come to dust

Cymbeline, IV.ii, lines 259–263

Strategy and Tactics

. . . and the dev'l hath power
T'assume a pleasing shape . . .

Hamlet, II.ii, lines 595–596

Till then 'tis wisdom to conceal our meaning
Henry VI, Part III, IV.viii, line 60

Have more than thou showest,
Speak less than thou knowest,
Lend less than thou owest,
Ride more than thou goest,
Learn more than thou trowest,
[trow = believe, think, know]
Set less than thou throwest [last line = stake less
than you risk on the throw of a dice]
King Lear, I.iv, lines 117–122

A little fire is quickly trodden out,
Which, being suffer'd, rivers cannot quench
Henry VI, Part III, IV.viii, lines 7–8

In cases of defence, 'tis best to weigh
The enemy more mighty than he seems
Henry V, II.iv, lines 43–44

. . . When we mean to build,
We first survey the plot, then draw the model;
And when we see the figure of the house,
Then must we rate the cost of the erection;
Which if we find outweighs ability,
What do we then but draw anew the model

In fewer offices, or at least desist
To build at all? . . .

Henry IV, Part II, I.iii, lines 40–47

. . . Beware
Of entrance to a quarrel; but, being in,
Bear't that th' opposed may beware of thee

Hamlet, I.iii, lines 65–67

Give every man thy ear but few thy voice;
Take each man's censure, but reserve thy
    judgment

Hamlet, I.iii, lines 68–69

. . . O, it is excellent
To have a giant's strength!
But it is tyrannous
To use it like a giant

Measure for Measure, II.ii, lines 107–109

Teamwork

We few, we happy few, we band of brothers

Henry V, IV.iii, line 60

All the world's a stage,
And all the men and women merely players;
They have their exits and their entrances;
And one man in his time plays many parts

As You Like It, II.vii, lines 139–142

Take but degree away, untune that string,
And hark what discord follows! . . .

Troilus and Cressida, I.iii, lines 109–110

His part is played, and though it were too
    short, he did it well

The Two Noble Kinsmen, I.iv, line 102

We few, we happy few, we band of brothers;
For he today that sheds his blood with me
Shall be my brother; be he ne'er so vile,
This day shall gentle his condition;
And gentlemen in England now a-bed
Shall think themselves accurs'd they were
    not here,
And hold their manhoods cheap whiles any
    speaks
That fought with us upon Saint Crispin's day

Henry V, IV.iii, lines 60–67

For doughty-handed are you, and have
    fought
Not as you serv'd the cause, but as't had
    been
Each man's like mine . . .

Antony and Cleopatra, IV.viii, lines 5–7

In them I trust, for they are soldiers
Witty, courteous, liberal, full of spirit

Henry VI Part III, I.ii, lines 42–43

Youth, Age and Experience

The oldest hath born most; we that are
    young
Shall never see so much, nor live so long

King Lear, V.iii, lines 325–326

. . . my thrice-puissant liege   [puissant = strong,
                 powerful] [liege = sovereign lord]
Is in the very May-morn of his youth,
Ripe for exploits and mighty enterprises

Henry V, I.ii, lines 119–121

My salad days,
When I was green in judgment . . .

Anthony and Cleopatra, I.v, lines 75–76

He jests at scars that never felt a wound

Romeo and Juliet, II.i, line 43

Young blood doth not obey an old decree

Love's Labours Lost, IV.iii, line 212

His years but young, but his experience old;
His head unmellowed, but his judgment ripe

The Two Gentlemen of Verona, II.iv, lines 65–66

Experience is by industry achiev'd,
And perfected by the swift course of time

The Two Gentlemen of Verona, I.iii, lines 22–23

. . . Superfluous branches
We lop away, that bearing boughs may live

Richard II, III.iv, lines 63–64

BIBLIOGRAPHY

Armstrong, Jane (comp.), *The Arden Shakespeare Book of Quotations on Life*, Thomson Learning, London, 2001

Bate, Jonathon, *The Genius of Shakespeare*, Picador, London, 1997

Bloom, Harold, *Shakespeare: The Invention of the Human*, Riverhead Books, New York, 1998

De Grazia, Margreta and Wells, Stanley (eds), *The Cambridge Companion to Shakespeare*, Cambridge University Press, Cambridge, 2001

Eagleson, Robert D., *A Shakespeare Glossary*, Oxford University Press, Oxford, 1986

Enright, Dominique (comp.), *The Wicked Wit of William Shakespeare*, Michael O'Mara Books, London, 2002

Epstein, Norrie, *The Friendly Shakespeare*, Penguin, New York, 1993

Laroque, Francois, *Shakespeare Court, Crowd and Playhouse*, Thames & Hudson, London, 1993

Macrone, Michael (ed.), *Shakespeare's Guide to Life: Truly Timeless Wisdom from the Plays and Sonnets*, HarperCollins, London, 1997

McLeish, K. and Unwin, S., *A Pocket Guide to Shakespeare's Plays*, Faber & Faber, London, 1998

Merton Babcock, C. (ed.), *Shakespeare Wisdom and Wit*, The Peter Pauper Press, New York, 1967

Wells, Stanley, *Shakespeare The Poet and His Plays*, Methuen, London, 1997

Wells, Stanley, *A Dictionary of Shakespeare*, Oxford University Press, Oxford, 1998

Wells, Stanley and Taylor, Gary (eds), *William Shakespeare: The Complete Works Compact Edition*, Clarendon Press, Oxford, 1988

Whitney, John O. and Packer, Tina, *Power Plays: Shakespeare's Lessons in Leadership and Management*, Simon & Schuster, New York, 2000

These two websites were very helpful:

The amazing website of Shakespeare's sonnets
www.shakespeares-sonnets.com

The Collected works of Shakespeare
www.it.usyd.edu.au/~matty/shapespeare

CHRONOLOGY OF
SHAKESPEARE'S WORKS

Work	Probable Date of Composition
King Henry VI, Part I	1589–1590
King Henry VI, Part II	1590–1591
King Henry VI, Part III	1590–1592
King Richard III	1592–1593
Venus and Adonis (poem)	1592–1593
The Comedy of Errors	1592–1594
The Two Gentlemen of Verona	1592–1594
Sonnets	Published in 1609 but in circulation in 1590s
The Rape of Lucrece (poem)	1593–1594
Titus Andronicus	1593–1594
The Taming of the Shrew	1593–1594
Love's Labour's Lost	1594–1595 (revised 1597)

Work	Probable Date of Composition
King John	1594–1596
King Richard II	1595
Romeo and Juliet	1595–1596
A Midsummer Night's Dream	1595–1596
The Merchant of Venice	1596–1597
King Henry IV, Part I	1596–1597
The Merry Wives of Windsor	1596–1599 (revised 1600–1601)
King Henry IV, Part II	1597–1598
Much Ado About Nothing	1598–1599
King Henry V	1599
Julius Caesar	1599
As You Like It	1599
Hamlet	1600–1601
The Phoenix and the Turtle (poem)	1601
Twelfth Night	1601–1602
Troilus and Cressida	1601–1602
A Lover's Complaint (poem)	1602–1608
All's Well That Ends Well	1602–1603
Measure for Measure	1604
Othello	1604
King Lear	1605
Macbeth	1606

Work	Probable Date of Composition
Antony and Cleopatra	1606–1607
Timon of Athens	1607–1608
Pericles	1607–1608
Coriolanus	1607–1609
Cymbeline	1609–1610
The Winter's Tale	1610–1611
The Tempest	1611
King Henry VIII	1611–1613
The Two Noble Kinsmen	1612–1613

ALSO BY RIC CHARLESWORTH AND AVAILABLE FROM PAN MACMILLAN

Ric Charlesworth
The Coach: Managing for Success

Ric Charlesworth confirmed his place as Australia's most successful coach after steering the Hockeyroos to back-to-back gold medal victories at the Atlanta and Sydney Olympics.

Taking the Hockeyroos' triumph at the 2000 Games as his starting point, Ric offers fascinating and useful insights into his innovative coaching philosophies. These ideas can be applied within and outside the sporting world to achieve success. His theories about co-operation and striving for excellence can be used by managers, business people and everyone who is working to reach a goal.

'*The Coach* takes you inside Ric's sports world. It's fascinating, extremely well planned and thought provoking – but then that is Ric's way. A must read for players and coaches regardless of your sport.'
WAYNE BENNETT, five times premiership coach for the Brisbane Broncos

'My reading round sporting performance, and in particular coaching, has been prolific . . . But none in my opinion do it better than *The Coach*.'
DAVID PARKIN, four times AFL premiership coach

Ric Charlesworth
Staying at the Top

Australia's most successful and innovative coach reveals how to maintain the success you've worked hard to achieve.

Ric Charlesworth coached the Hockeyroos to number one world ranking in 1993, where they stayed for 8 years, winning Olympic gold twice in that time.

Staying at the Top offers a unique insight into the practices and methods of a great team and its coach. Charlesworth gives his readers his five principles for establishing a winning culture, whether it be in sport or business. Then – and most importantly – he outlines how to 'stay there'. He identifies the pitfalls of success and the practices which ensure that quality can always be improved, refreshed, redefined and maintained.

Many books have been written on how to achieve success. This unique account describes how a great team can work to maintain the top spot. The messages and the approach are as relevant to business leadership and management as they are to sport.